P9-CRN-379

Authentic Family-Style

MEXICAN
COOKING

Every day, families create and share good times at the dinner table. Great food and good conversation bring busy lives into focus and draw everyone together. Special meals often become memories that pass from generation to generation.

One family whose mealtime memories span 100 years is the Ortega family, pioneers in the food industry. Since 1897, the Ortega name has symbolized authentic, family-style Mexican food. Moreover, Ortega is synonymous with one of the most important staples of Mexican cuisine— green chiles. Over the last 100 years, countless family announcements, birthdays and everyday events have been happily shared over a plate of chiles rellenos and other dishes flavored with Ortega products.

In celebration of Ortega's 100th anniversary, this limited-edition cookbook has been created to preserve the rich heritage and colorful legacy of the Ortega family. Your family will enjoy this collection of authentic Mexican recipes, special Ortega family stories, historic photographs and helpful cooking tips.

The book's introductory historical narrative was written by best-selling author Victor Villaseñor, who spent more than 10 years researching his own roots and his family's incredible journey from Mexico to the United States. In the pages that follow, Mr. Villaseñor recounts the bold history of Ortega's founder, the pioneering entrepreneur Emilio C. Ortega, and his family. Since the company's beginnings a century ago, the Ortega name has grown to symbolize authentic Mexican foods that bring families together.

Welcome to our celebration of 100 years of great Mexican meals. Discover Ortega's vibrant history and proud heritage, and try the delicious recipes especially selected for this book. By sharing some of our mealtime favorites, we hope to inspire you to create warm memories around the table with your own family.

Pictured on front cover: *Chicken Enchiladas with Pickled Vegetables* (recipe, page 36).

© Copyright 1997 Nestlé.   Introduction and Historical Narrative © Victor Villaseñor.   Contributing Food Photographer: Myron Beck. Special thanks to the Ortega family and friends for their contributions to the writing of this book.

All rights reserved. Produced by Meredith Custom Publishing, 1912 Grand Ave., Des Moines, Iowa, 50309-3379. Library of Congress Catalog Card Number 97-070771. ISBN 0-696-20697-8. Canadian GST Reg # BN 12348 2887 RT. Printed in the U.S.A.

CONTENTS

100 Years of Family Traditions 4-19

A century ago, Emilio C. Ortega's passion for chiles
inspired him to create a food company to share his love of good
food with families all over the country.

A Century of Ortega Classics 20-45

A Yucatán Feast 22-27
Classic Chicken Dinner 28-33
Ortega Family Favorites 34-37
Ortega Heritage Dinner 38-41
Mexican-Style Brunch 42-45

Great Meals with Great Friends 46-67

Festive Fajita Dinner 48-51
Spicy Dinner 52-55
Ranch-Style Supper 56-59
Special Dinner Celebration 60-63
Soup Supper 64-67

One-Dish Dinners 68-77

Enchilada Dinner 70-71
Salad Lunch 72-73
Casserole Supper 74-75
Skillet Chicken Dinner 76
Chimichanga Supper 77

Quick & Easy Mexican Cooking 78-103

Taco Dinner 80-83
Family-Pleasing Burritos 84-87
Tostada Supper 88-91
Warming Soup Supper 92-95
Vegetarian Fajita Dinner 96-99
Vegetarian Enchilada Dinner 100-103

Accent on the Holidays 104-125

Fiesta Navideña 106-113
Holiday Brunch 114-119
Cinco de Mayo Fiesta 120-125

100 Years of Family Tradition

Emilio C. Ortega

THE EARLY YEARS

Emilio C. Ortega, the founder of the Pioneer Ortega Chile Packing Company of Los Angeles, started his chile roasting and canning business in the little adobe house where he was born in Ventura, California.

His parents didn't have much money, but they always had plenty of great food and exciting stories to share at the dinner table with Emilio and his 13 brothers and sisters.

The twelfth child in his family, Emilio was raised on spicy Mexican food and equally spicy stories of local pirates and Indians. He also learned how his ancestors had come from Spain to Guadalajara, Mexico, and then to Baja, California. His great grandfather, José Francisco Ortega, had actually been on the expedition with Don Gaspar Portola, the Spanish explorer credited with discovering the San Francisco Bay.

idays

Holidays in Mexico are known for their joyfulness.
From homemade, traditional Christmas tamales to a
patriotic Cinco de Mayo feast, there is no better way
to create joy than by sharing a festive holiday meal
with your loved ones.

Enrich your holidays with this authentic

Mexican Christmas repast. Select one of three different fillings

for these traditional tamales. Then, top off the festivities with decadent

bread pudding and hot chocolate.

Fiesta Navideña

Ortega Green Chile Guacamole with Tortilla Chips
(recipe page 123)

Tamales

Zucchini with Green Chiles

Marinated Vegetable Salad

Mocha Bread Pudding with Caramel Sauce

Mexican Hot Chocolate

Tamales with Shredded Pork Filling,
Shredded Beef Filling and Shredded Chicken Filling
(recipes pages 108 and 109)

Tamales

For a fanciful touch, secure the tamales with long strips of green onion.

> 4 to 5 cups Shredded Beef, Pork or Chicken Filling (see recipes below and opposite page)
> 1 package (8 ounces) dried corn husks
> ⅔ cup lard or shortening
> 4 cups masa harina flour (Mexican corn masa mix)
> 2 teaspoons salt
> 3 cups broth from filling or water
> ⅓ cup lard or shortening, melted

SORT corn husks, setting aside any torn ones. Soak intact husks in warm water for at least 1 hour or until softened and easy to fold.

BEAT ⅔ *cup* lard in large mixer bowl until creamy. Combine flour and salt in medium bowl. Alternately add flour mixture and broth to lard, mixing well after each addition. Gradually add *melted* lard, mixing until consistency of thick cake batter (masa). Spread ¼ cup masa, using back of a spoon, to form a square in the center of one husk. Place about ¼ cup meat filling in center of masa square. Fold right then left edge of husk over masa. Fold up bottom edge. Repeat with remaining ingredients.

PLACE vegetable steamer in pot with lid; add water to just below steamer. Arrange tamales upright in steamer rack. Cover top of tamales with reserved dry husks and a damp towel; cover. Bring to a boil; reduce heat to low. Steam, adding water as needed, for 2 to 2½ hours or until masa pulls away from husks. Makes about 2 dozen.

Shredded Beef Filling

MACHACA

Double this versatile recipe and freeze half to have on hand for a quick burrito filling.

> 2 quarts water
> 3 pounds boneless beef shoulder clod or chuck roast
> 1 small onion, quartered
> 2 tablespoons vegetable oil
> 1 cup (1 small) chopped onion
> ½ cup chopped red and/or green bell pepper
> 1 cup ORTEGA Green Chile Picante Sauce, medium or mild
> ¼ cup chopped fresh cilantro
> 1 tablespoon ORTEGA Diced Jalapeños

COMBINE water, beef and quartered onion in large stockpot. Bring to a boil. Reduce heat to medium-low. Cook, covered, for 1½ to 2 hours or until meat is very tender. Remove beef. Strain broth; reserve *1 cup* for meat filling (remaining broth may be refrigerated or frozen for future use). Shred beef.

HEAT oil in large skillet over medium-high heat. Add chopped onion and bell pepper; cook, stirring occasionally, for 2 to 3 minutes or until vegetables are tender. Add shredded meat, *reserved* broth, picante sauce, cilantro and jalapeños. Cook, stirring occasionally, for 4 to 5 minutes or until heated through.

USE filling in burritos, tacos, tostadas or tamales. Makes 5 cups.

Shredded Pork Filling

RELLENO DE CERDO

Mexican cooked pork is known for its succulence. It is used in chorizo (spicy sausage), meatballs and many of Mexico's savory fillings.

> 4 **cups water**
> 2 **pounds boneless pork butt or pork roast**
> 1 **small onion, quartered**
> 1 **teaspoon salt**
> 1 **tablespoon vegetable oil**
> 1 **cup (1 small) chopped onion**
> 3 **cloves garlic, finely chopped**
> 1 **cup (7-ounce can) ORTEGA Diced Green Chiles**
> 1½ **to 2 teaspoons ground oregano**
>   **Salt and ground black pepper to taste**

COMBINE water, pork, quartered onion and salt in large stockpot. Bring to a boil. Reduce heat to low. Cook, covered, for 1½ to 2 hours or until meat is very tender. Remove pork. Strain broth; reserve ½ cup for meat filling (remaining broth may be refrigerated or frozen for future use). Shred pork.

HEAT oil in large skillet over medium-high heat. Add chopped onion, garlic and shredded pork; cook, stirring occasionally, for 3 to 4 minutes or until onion is tender. Stir in *reserved* broth, chiles, oregano, salt and pepper. Cook, stirring occasionally, for 4 to 5 minutes or until heated through.

USE filling in burritos, tacos, tostadas or tamales. Makes 4 cups.

Shredded Chicken Filling

RELLENO DE POLLO

Tomatillos, Mexican green tomatoes, add a citrusy flavor to this savory filling.

> 2 **pounds chicken breast meat, cooked, shredded**
> 1 **pound tomatillos, husks removed, boiled for 4 to 5 minutes**
> 1 **cup (7-ounce can) ORTEGA Diced Green Chiles**
> 2 **large cloves garlic, peeled**
> 1 **teaspoon salt**
> 1 **tablespoon oil**
> 1 **cup (1 small) chopped onion**
> 2 **teaspoons chopped fresh cilantro**

COMBINE tomatillos, chiles, garlic and salt in food processor or blender container; cover. Process for 1 minute or until mixture is smooth.

HEAT oil in large skillet over medium-high heat. Add onion; cook, stirring occasionally, for 1 to 2 minutes or until onion is tender. Stir in tomatillo mixture and chicken. Cook, stirring occasionally, for 4 to 5 minutes or until heated through. Remove from heat; stir in cilantro.

USE as a filling in burritos, tacos, enchiladas or tamales. Makes 4½ cups.

Shredded Meat

Unlike in the United States—where ground meat is popularly used in Mexican foods—traditional preparation of meat in Mexico calls for cooked meat to be shredded to make fillings for any number of stuffed foods such as tacos, enchiladas or chiles rellenos.

Whether it's chicken, pork or beef, meat can be stewed, baked, boiled, broiled or grilled before it's shredded. Simply let it cool enough to handle, then pull the meat from the bone (if there is one) and shred it with two forks to the coarseness you desire.

Zucchini with Green Chiles
CALABACITAS CON CHILES VERDES

Mild zucchini, crookneck squash and chiles unite to brighten the holiday table.

- 2 tablespoons vegetable oil
- 3 cups (3 large) sliced green zucchini
- 2 cups (2 medium) sliced yellow crookneck squash or yellow zucchini
- 1 cup (1 small) sliced onion
- 2 cloves garlic, finely chopped
- 1 cup (1 medium) chopped tomato
- 1 cup (7-ounce can) ORTEGA Diced Green Chiles
- ½ teaspoon salt

HEAT oil in large skillet over medium-high heat. Add zucchini, squash, onion and garlic; cook, stirring occasionally, for 3 to 5 minutes or until vegetables are tender. Add tomato, chiles and salt; cook for 1 minute or until heated through. Makes 12 servings.

Marinated Vegetable Salad
ENSALADA DE VEGETALES MARINADAS

Typical of Mexican salads, this comforting combination of crisp vegetables is dressed with lime juice, olive oil and fresh herbs.

- ¾ cup ORTEGA Thick & Chunky Salsa, hot, medium or mild
- ¼ cup lime juice
- ¼ cup chopped fresh parsley or cilantro
- 2 tablespoons olive oil
- 2 cups (2 medium) chopped tomatoes
- 2 cups (2 medium) chopped zucchini
- 1½ cups (15-ounce can) kidney beans, rinsed, drained
- 1 medium ripe avocado, peeled, seeded and chopped
- ½ cup (4-ounce can) ORTEGA Diced Green Chiles
- 12 cups (1 medium head) chopped lettuce leaves

COMBINE salsa, lime juice, parsley and oil in large bowl.

ADD tomatoes, zucchini, kidney beans, avocado and chiles. Toss well to coat. Cover; chill for at least 2 hours.

PLACE 1 cup lettuce on each salad plate; top with ½ cup vegetable mixture. Makes 12 servings.

Mexican Hot Chocolate
CHAMPURRADO

Christmas in Mexico

For the most authentic flavor, buy piloncillo (unrefined sugar) which has a molasses-like taste. Piloncillo cones are available at most Mexican or Latin American markets. Chop the cones into small pieces with a serrated knife before using.

- **12 cups water, *divided***
- **3 cinnamon sticks**
- **1½ cups masa harina flour (Mexican corn masa mix)**
- **1½ cups packed brown sugar or 2 large (6 ounces *each*) piloncillo cones (Mexican brown sugar)**
- **1 ounce *(half* 2-ounce bar) NESTLÉ TOLL HOUSE Unsweetened Chocolate Baking Bar**
- **2 teaspoons vanilla extract**

COMBINE *8 cups* water and cinnamon in large saucepan. Bring to a boil.

PLACE *remaining* water and flour in blender container; cover. Blend until smooth. Pour mixture through fine-mesh sieve into cinnamon-water mixture. Bring to a boil. Reduce heat to low; cook, stirring constantly with wire whisk, for 6 to 7 minutes or until mixture is thickened.

STIR in sugar, chocolate and vanilla. Cook, stirring frequently, for 4 to 5 minutes or until chocolate is melted and flavors are blended. Makes 12 servings.

Cornmeal and Corn Flour

Corn in all of its guises is central to Mexican cookery—particularly cornmeal and the dried-corn flour called masa harina, which is used to make tortillas.

White or yellow cornmeal and masa harina are both made from dried field corn rather than sweet corn, but the similarities end there. Cornmeal is simply ground, dried corn. To make masa, however, dried corn is boiled with pickling or mason's lime to dissolve the outer hulls of the kernels. The corn is then rinsed thoroughly, and stone-ground into a paste (finely ground for tortillas and coarsely ground for tamales).

Traditionally, the fresh masa was hand-patted (for the most tender tortillas) and griddle-baked into the fragrant flatbreads.

Mexicans have a long, rich tradition of celebrating Christmas with gusto. Homes are decorated with white lilies, Spanish moss, evergreens and paper lanterns called luminarias. Instead of decorating a Christmas tree, Mexicans break a piñata each of the nine nights before Christmas. Every child is blindfolded and gets three chances to break the piñata with a heavy stick. The fragile clay or papier-maché shape, covered in brightly colored tissue paper and tinsel, is filled with nuts, candies and small toys for the children—and the young at heart—to scramble after when the piñata breaks.

And what would Christmas be without its traditional foods? The best known are tamales, made in abundance all over Mexico.

Mocha Bread Pudding with Caramel Sauce

Pudín de Moca con Salsa de Caramelo

A great way to use day-old bread, this luscious pudding combines the favorite Mexican flavors of chocolate and coffee, to make a first-class finale.

Bread Pudding

- 9 cups (about 1-pound loaf) 1-inch cubes French bread
- 1 cup granulated sugar
- ¼ cup NESTLÉ TOLL HOUSE Baking Cocoa
- 1 tablespoon TASTER'S CHOICE Original Blend Freeze Dried Coffee
- 4 eggs
- 3 cups (*two* 12 fluid-ounce cans) CARNATION Evaporated Skimmed Milk or Evaporated Lowfat Milk, *divided*
- 2 teaspoons vanilla extract

Caramel Sauce

- ⅔ cup packed brown sugar
- ¼ cup (½ stick) butter or margarine
- 1 tablespoon light corn syrup

For Bread Pudding:

PLACE bread cubes in greased 2-quart baking dish. Combine sugar, cocoa and coffee granules in small bowl.

BEAT eggs, *2⅔ cups* evaporated milk and vanilla in medium bowl until well blended; stir in sugar mixture. Pour over bread, pressing bread into milk mixture.

BAKE in preheated 350°F. oven for 50 to 55 minutes or until set.

For Caramel Sauce:

COMBINE brown sugar, butter and corn syrup in small saucepan. Cook over medium-low heat, stirring constantly, for 2 to 3 minutes or until sugar is dissolved. Slowly stir in *remaining* evaporated milk. Bring to a boil, stirring constantly; cook for 1 minute. Remove from heat. Serve with warm bread pudding. Makes 12 servings.

Mocha Bread Pudding with Caramel Sauce

Whatever the occasion—Christmas, Easter, Mother's Day

or a birthday—brunch is the perfect way to celebrate.

Make the meal especially memorable with this delightful assortment

of Mexican dishes. From the savory quiche to the irresistible

fruit chimichangas, your guests will enjoy every bite.

Holiday Brunch

Sausage Quiche

Fresh-Fruit Platter

Assorted Breads

Golden Pound Cake
~ or ~
Fruit-Filled Chimichangas with Cinnamon Custard Sauce

Orange Juice

Mexican Hot Cocoa

Sausage Quiche
(recipe page 116)

Sausage Quiche

Chorizo is a highly seasoned pork sausage with a deep red color. If you can't find it, try using Polish kielbasa, Cajun smoked andouille or spicy pork sausage instead.

    1 teaspoon vegetable oil
    1 (12-inch) burrito-size flour tortilla
    5 ounces longaniza-style chorizo, casing removed, crumbled, or 6 ounces
       breakfast sausage
    ½ cup ORTEGA Thick & Chunky Salsa, mild
    5 eggs
    ½ cup half-and-half or whole milk
    1 cup (4 ounces) shredded Monterey Jack cheese
    1 tablespoon chopped fresh cilantro
       ORTEGA Thick & Chunky Salsa, mild (optional)

HEAT oil in large skillet over medium-high heat. Place tortilla in skillet. Cook for 1 minute on each side or until golden and slightly crisp. Place tortilla on bottom of lightly greased 9-inch pie plate. Add chorizo to skillet; cook over medium-high heat, stirring frequently, for 3 to 4 minutes or until cooked through; drain. Spoon ½ cup salsa over tortilla; top with chorizo.

COMBINE eggs and half-and-half in small bowl; add cheese and cilantro. Pour egg mixture over chorizo.

BAKE in preheated 375°F. oven for 25 to 30 minutes or until knife inserted in center comes out clean. Cool for 5 minutes on wire rack. Cut into wedges; serve with salsa.
Makes 6 servings.

Buying Mexican Cheese

Cheeses of all tastes and textures are integral to Mexican cooking. They are used with a generous hand for stuffing and topping.

Queso fresco is a generic term for fresh cheese. In Mexico, fresh cheeses are soft, white and crumbly. They are meant to be sprinkled over tacos, tostadas and other dishes featuring tortillas. If you can't find a queso fresco, substitute a mild feta.

Queso añejo (aged cheese) is a hard cheese that is grated and used as a topping, much like Parmesan cheese. Cotija is one example of an aged cheese. If you can't find that, substitute a dry farmer's cheese, Parmesan or a dry feta cheese.

For stuffing chiles, quesadillas and other dishes, firm but meltable cheeses are desirable. If you can't find a melting Mexican cheese, try mozzarella, muenster or Monterey Jack cheese—or a combination.

Mexican Hot Cocoa

COCOA MEXICANA

In Mexico, chocolate is most often consumed as a warm beverage, accented with cinnamon and vanilla.

- ½ cup granulated sugar
- ½ cup NESTLÉ TOLL HOUSE Baking Cocoa
- ¾ teaspoon ground cinnamon
- 6 cups milk
- 2 teaspoons vanilla extract

COMBINE sugar, cocoa and cinnamon in small saucepan; gradually stir in milk. Warm over medium heat, stirring constantly, until hot (do not boil). Remove from heat; stir in vanilla. Beat with wire whisk until frothy. Makes 6 servings.

NOTE: Mexican Hot Cocoa may also be prepared with ABUELITA Authentic Mexican Chocolate Drink Mix. Chop 1½ tablets (about 5 ounces) in blender container or food processor. Add 6 cups hot milk; process until smooth.

Golden Pound Cake

PANQUÉ DORADO

Mexican cakes are typically simple to bake, richly-flavored and scented with vanilla. For a special touch, serve slices of this cake with Cinnamon Custard Sauce (see page 119).

- 3 cups cake flour or 2⅔ cups all-purpose flour
- 1½ teaspoons baking powder
- ¼ teaspoon salt
- ¼ teaspoon ground mace or ground nutmeg
- 1½ cups granulated sugar
- 1 cup (2 sticks) butter or margarine, softened
- 1 teaspoon vanilla extract
- 3 eggs
- ½ cup CARNATION Evaporated Milk
- ¾ cup chopped walnuts or pecans

COMBINE flour, baking powder, salt and mace in medium bowl. Beat sugar, butter and vanilla in large mixer bowl until light and fluffy. Add eggs one at a time, beating well after each addition.

ADD flour mixture alternately with evaporated milk, beating well after each addition. Pour into greased 9 x 5-inch loaf pan; sprinkle with nuts.

BAKE in preheated 350° F. oven for 60 to 70 minutes or until wooden pick inserted near center comes out clean. Cool in pan on wire rack for 10 minutes. Remove to wire rack to cool completely. Makes 12 servings.

Mexican Holidays

Every day is one to celebrate in sunny Mexico, but certain days are held especially dear.

One of the most enthusiastically observed holidays is All Soul's Day (November 2), when families pay respect to their deceased relatives by bringing food offerings to their graves. They bake a special bread, called pan de muerto (bread for the dead), rich with eggs and flavored with orange peel and orange extract.

A few weeks later, the Christmas celebration starts and doesn't truly end until January 6, also known as Epiphany or Three King's Day, the day the Christ Child was revealed to the Magi. On the night before Three King's Day, children put their shoes in the window to be filled with presents.

Fruit-Filled Chimichangas with Cinnamon Custard Sauce

CHIMICHANGAS DE FRUTA CON SALSA DE CANELA

Best when served warm, these dessert chimichangas can be made with any combination of your favorite dried fruits.

Cinnamon Custard Sauce
- ⅓ cup granulated sugar
- 2 teaspoons cornstarch
- ½ teaspoon ground cinnamon
- 1 cup CARNATION Evaporated Milk
- ⅓ cup water
- 1 egg yolk, lightly beaten
- 1 teaspoon vanilla extract

Chimichangas
- 1½ cups water
- 1 cup (6 ounces) dried apricots, chopped
- 1 cup (3 ounces) dried apples, chopped
- ¾ cup chopped nuts
- ½ cup granulated sugar
- ½ teaspoon ground cinnamon
- 12 (8-inch) soft taco-size flour tortillas, warmed
- Vegetable oil
- Powdered sugar (optional)
- Fresh mint leaves (optional)

For Cinnamon Custard Sauce:
COMBINE sugar, cornstarch and cinnamon in medium saucepan; gradually stir in evaporated milk, water and egg yolk. Bring to a boil over medium heat, stirring constantly, until mixture is slightly thickened. Remove from heat; stir in vanilla. Cover; keep warm.

For Chimichangas:
COMBINE water, apricots, apples, nuts, sugar and cinnamon in medium saucepan. Bring to a boil. Reduce heat to medium; cover. Cook, stirring occasionally, for 10 to 15 minutes or until excess moisture is absorbed. Cool for 15 minutes.

PLACE ¼ cup fruit mixture in center of each tortilla. Fold into burritos (see tip page 86); secure ends with wooden picks. Add oil to 1-inch depth in medium skillet; heat over high heat for 3 to 4 minutes. Place 2 or 3 chimichangas at a time in oil; fry, turning frequently with tongs, for 1 to 2 minutes or until golden brown. Place on paper towels to soak. Remove wooden picks. Sprinkle with powdered sugar. Serve with Cinnamon Custard Sauce. Garnish with mint. Makes 12 servings.

Get into the spirit of spring with an informal
Cinco de Mayo (fifth of May) celebration. Guacamole, hearty tacos
and burritos and rich chocolate cake served for dessert
enhance the festivities.

Cinco de Mayo Fiesta

Ortega Green Chile Guacamole

Original Ortega Tacos

Chicken and Bean Burritos

Mexican Rice
(recipe page 51)

Ortega Refried Beans

Cinnamon Chocolate Cake

Sparkling Fruit Punch

Original Ortega Tacos (recipe page 122)
Mexican Rice (recipe page 51)

Original Ortega Tacos
LA RECTA DE TACOS ORIGINALES ORTEGA

Build-your-own tacos are a treat that brings the whole family to the table. Entice everyone with a variety of toppings, such as sliced radishes, olives, avocados and Ortega Taco Sauce.

- 1 pound ground beef
- 1 package (1.25 ounces) ORTEGA Taco Seasoning Mix
- ¾ cup water
- 1 package (12) ORTEGA Taco Shells or (12) ORTEGA White Corn Taco Shells, warmed
- 2½ cups torn lettuce
- 2 cups (2 medium) chopped tomatoes
- 1½ cups (6 ounces) shredded cheese
- ORTEGA Green Chile Guacamole (recipe opposite page)
- ORTEGA Thick & Smooth Taco Sauce, hot, medium or mild
- Additional Topping Suggestions: chopped onion, chopped green bell pepper, sour cream, sliced avocado and sliced ripe olives

COOK beef in medium skillet over medium-high heat, stirring occasionally, for 4 to 5 minutes or until no longer pink; drain. Stir in taco seasoning mix and water. Bring to a boil. Reduce heat to low; cook, stirring occasionally, for 5 to 6 minutes or until thickened.

FILL taco shells with 2 to 3 tablespoons beef mixture. Top with lettuce, tomatoes, cheese, guacamole, taco sauce and additional topping suggestions. Makes 12 servings.

Chicken and Bean Burritos
BURRITOS DE POLLO Y FRIJOLES

Boneless, skinless chicken breast and fat-free refried beans make these hearty burritos guilt-free eating.

- 1 tablespoon vegetable oil
- 1 pound boneless, skinless chicken breast meat, cut into strips
- 1 package (1.5 ounces) ORTEGA Burrito Seasoning Mix
- 1 cup water
- 1¾ cups (1-pound can) ORTEGA Fat Free Refried Beans
- 8 (10-inch) burrito-size flour tortillas, warmed
- 2 cups shredded lettuce
- 1 cup (4 ounces) shredded Monterey Jack or cheddar cheese
- ½ cup (about 4 large) sliced green onions

HEAT oil in large skillet over medium-high heat. Add chicken; cook, stirring constantly, for 4 to 5 minutes or until no longer pink. Stir in burrito seasoning mix and water. Bring to a boil. Reduce heat to low; cook, stirring occasionally, for 3 to 4 minutes or until mixture is thickened. Stir in beans; cook for 1 to 2 minutes or until heated through.

PLACE ½ cup chicken mixture on each tortilla. Top each with ¼ cup lettuce, 2 tablespoons cheese and 1 tablespoon green onion; fold into burritos (see tip page 86). Makes 8 servings.

Ortega Green Chile Guacamole
GUACAMOLE CON CHILES VERDES ORTEGA

Green chiles add a boost of flavor to the Ortega-family version of this ever-popular dip. Serve it with tortilla chips and crisp slices of jicama, cucumber and radish.

- 2 medium, very ripe avocados, seeded, peeled and mashed
- ½ cup (4-ounce can) ORTEGA Diced Green Chiles
- ⅓ cup (about 2 large) chopped green onions
- 2 tablespoons olive oil
- 1 teaspoon lime juice
- 1 clove garlic, finely chopped
- ¼ teaspoon salt
- Tortilla chips

COMBINE avocados, chiles, green onions, oil, lime juice, garlic and salt in medium bowl. Cover; chill for at least 1 hour. Serve with chips. Makes about 2 cups.

Avocados

A fruit native to Mexico, velvety avocados appear in many forms in Mexican cuisine, but most frequently in guacamole. If you want fresh guacamole, it takes a little planning: Avocados are one of the few fruits that don't actually ripen on the tree. In fact, they don't ripen until they're in a warm place, so it's unlikely you'll even find a perfectly ripe avocado in the grocery store.

Buy firm avocados if you won't be using them for a few days. They'll ripen in 3 to 4 days (you can speed the process by placing avocados in a brown paper bag). Don't buy avocados with dark spots or broken skin.

You can tell an avocado is ripe when it yields to gentle pressure. Give the avocado a gentle shake. If you can hear the seed rattling around inside, the fruit is overripe.

To prevent avocado garnishes from turning brown, brush the cut surfaces with lemon juice.

Cinco de Mayo commemorates the unlikely victory by a group of Mexican soldiers against the professional troops of French Emperor Napoléon III on May 5, 1862, at the city of Puebla. Napoléon had invaded Mexico during a civil war to capitalize on its instability. The Mexican soldiers not only held Puebla, they forced Napoléon's troops to retreat.

In the United States, it is often assumed that Cinco de Mayo (the Fifth of May) is, like our Fourth of July, an Independence Day. In truth, the Mexican Independence Day is celebrated on September 16, but Cinco de Mayo gets as much fanfare.

Cinco de Mayo is a patriotic holiday, celebrated with mariachi music, dancing, military parades, speeches, piñatas and great food.

In particular, foods featuring the colors of the Mexican flag are favored. For a cuisine awash in red and green chiles, tomatoes, rice and white cheeses, that is not a difficult cooking feat to accomplish.

Cinnamon Chocolate Cake

BIZCOCHO DE CHOCOLATE Y CANELA

In this rich, intriguing cake, the complementary flavors of cinnamon and chocolate heat up with the addition of one surprise ingredient: jalapeños.

Chocolate Cake
- 1 cup (6-ounce package) NESTLÉ TOLL HOUSE Semi-Sweet Chocolate Morsels, melted, cooled
- 1¼ cups granulated sugar
- ¾ cup (1½ sticks) butter or margarine, softened
- 1 teaspoon vanilla extract
- 3 eggs
- 2 cups all-purpose flour
- 1 tablespoon ground cinnamon
- 1 teaspoon baking soda
- ½ teaspoon salt
- 1 cup milk
- 1 to 2 tablespoons ORTEGA Diced Jalapeños (optional)

Chocolate Frosting
- 3 to 3¼ cups sifted powdered sugar
- ⅓ cup milk
- ¼ cup (½ stick) butter or margarine, softened
- 2 packets (1 ounce *each*) NESTLÉ TOLL HOUSE CHOCO BAKE Unsweetened Chocolate Flavor
- 2 teaspoons vanilla extract
- ¼ teaspoon salt
- 1¾ cups sliced almonds, toasted

For Chocolate Cake:
BEAT granulated sugar, butter and vanilla in large mixer bowl. Add eggs; beat for 1 minute. Beat in melted morsels. Combine flour, cinnamon, baking soda and salt in medium bowl; beat into chocolate mixture alternately with milk. Stir in jalapeños. Pour into two well-greased 9-inch-round baking pans or one 13 x 9-inch baking pan.

BAKE in preheated 350°F. oven for 30 to 35 minutes or until wooden pick inserted in center comes out clean. Cool in pan(s) for 20 minutes; invert onto wire rack(s) to cool completely.

For Chocolate Frosting:
BEAT powdered sugar, milk, butter, chocolate flavor, vanilla and salt in small mixer bowl until mixture is smooth and creamy. Frost cake. Decorate sides with nuts. Makes 12 servings.

Index

Appetizers
Ortega Family Green Chile Dip, 51
Ortega Green Chile Guacamole, 123
Sopes, 26
Tostaditas with Fiesta Salsa, 31
Avocado and Green Chile Soup, 40

Baja Fish Tacos, 81
Beans (see also Refried Beans)
Cowboy Beans, 59
Marinated Vegetable Salad, 110
Ortega-Style Green Beans, 31
Vegetarian Fajitas, 98
Beef
Beef Chimichangas, 58
Burritos Grandes, 87
Carne Asada Burritos, 86
Cowboy Beans, 59
Enchilada Casserole, 71
Fajita-Style Beef Soft Tacos, 82
Meatballs in Chile Sauce, 54
Meatloaf Mexicana, 55
Mexican Taco Salad, 72
Original Burrito, The, 87
Original Ortega Tacos, 122
Shredded Beef Filling, 108
Shredded Beef with Eggs and
    Tortillas, 45
Tamale Pie, 74
Tamales, 108
Beverages
Mexican Hot Chocolate, 111
Mexican Hot Cocoa, 117
Mexican Milk Drink, 45
Breads
Fiesta Corn Bread, 66
Spoon Bread with Green
    Chiles, 63
Burritos
Burritos Grandes, 87
Carne Asada Burritos, 86
Chicken and Bean Burritos, 122
Original Burrito, The, 87

Caesar Salad with Cilantro and Green
    Chile Dressing, 24
Cakes
Cinnamon Chocolate Cake, 125
Golden Pound Cake, 117
Caramel Sauce, Mocha Bread Pudding
    with, 113
Carne Asada Burritos, 86

Cheese
Beef Chimichangas, 58
Burritos Grandes, 87
Caesar Salad with Cilantro and
    Green Chile Dressing, 24
Chicken and Bean Burritos, 122
Chicken Enchiladas with Pickled
    Vegetables, 36
Chilaquiles, 99
Creamy Bean Soup, 95
Enchilada Casserole, 71
Enchilada Stacks, 71
Fajita Quesadillas, 94
Fiesta Corn Bread, 66
Green Chile Quesadillas, 94
Grilled Chicken with Chile Strips
    in Cream, 26
Meatloaf Mexicana, 55
Mexican Taco Salad, 72
Original Burrito, The, 87
Original Ortega Tacos, 122
Ortega Chicken Fajitas, 50
Ortega Ranch-Style Eggs, 44
Refried Bean Tostadas, 91
Sausage Quiche, 116
Shredded Beef with Eggs and
    Tortillas, 45
Shrimp Enchiladas, 70
Shrimp Tostadas, 90
Sopes, 26
Spicy Tomato and Corn Soup, 95
Spinach and Mushroom
    Enchiladas, 102
Spoon Bread with Green Chiles, 63
Stuffed Chiles in Ranch Sauce, 25
Tamale Pie, 74
Tostaditas with Fiesta Salsa, 31
Turkey Tacos, 83
Chicken
Chicken and Bean Burritos, 122
Chicken and Hominy Soup, 66
Chicken Enchiladas with Pickled
    Vegetables, 36
Chicken in Stewed Tomato Sauce, 76
Chicken Mole, 62
Chicken with Rice, 30
Fajita Quesadillas, 94
Garden-Style Chicken
    Chimichangas, 77
Grilled Chicken with Chile Strips in
    Cream, 26
Ortega Chicken Fajitas, 50

Chicken *continued*
Shredded Chicken Filling, 109
Tamales, 108
Tortilla, Green Chile and Lime
    Soup, 40
Vermicelli Soup, 67
Chilaquiles, 99
Chimichangas
Beef Chimichangas, 58
Fruit-Filled Chimichangas with
    Cinnamon Custard Sauce, 119
Garden-Style Chicken
    Chimichangas, 77
Chocolate
Chocolate Chip Mexican Wedding
    Cakes, 27
Cinnamon Chocolate Cake, 125
Cinnamon Chocolate Pudding, 55
Mexican Hot Chocolate, 111
Mexican Hot Cocoa, 117
Mocha Bread Pudding with Caramel
    Sauce, 113
Cilantro and Green Chile
    Dressing, Caesar Salad with, 24
Cinnamon Chocolate Cake, 125
Cinnamon Chocolate Pudding, 55
Cinnamon Custard Sauce, Fruit-Filled
    Chimichangas with, 119
Corn
Corn with Tomatoes and Green
    Chiles, 63
Garden-Style Chicken
    Chimichangas, 77
Green Chile Quesadillas, 94
Mexicali Corn Salsa, 82
Spicy Tomato and Corn Soup, 95
Tamale Pie, 74
Tostaditas with Fiesta Salsa, 31
Vegetarian Fajitas, 98
Cowboy Beans, 59
Cream Cheese Flan, 33
Creamy Bean Soup, 95

Desserts (see also Cakes)
Chocolate Chip Mexican Wedding
    Cakes, 27
Cinnamon Chocolate Pudding, 55
Cream Cheese Flan, 33
Fruit-Filled Chimichangas with
    Cinnamon Custard Sauce, 119
Mocha Bread Pudding with Caramel
    Sauce, 113

Eggs
  Ortega Ranch-Style Eggs, 44
  Sausage Quiche, 116
  Shredded Beef with Eggs and
    Tortillas, 45
Enchiladas
  Chicken Enchiladas with Pickled
    Vegetables, 36
  Enchilada Casserole, 71
  Enchilada Stacks, 71
  Shrimp Enchiladas, 70
  Spinach and Mushroom
    Enchiladas, 102

Fajita Quesadillas, 94
Fajitas
  Ortega Chicken Fajitas, 50
  Vegetarian Fajitas, 98
Fajita-Style Beef Soft Tacos, 82
Fiesta Corn Bread, 66
Fiesta Salsa, 31
Fillings
  Shredded Beef Filling, 108
  Shredded Chicken Filling, 109
  Shredded Pork Filling, 109
Fish
  Baja Fish Tacos, 81
  Fish Veracruz, 41
Flan, Cream Cheese, 33
Fruit-Filled Chimichangas with
  Cinnamon Custard Sauce, 119

Garden-Style Chicken
  Chimichangas, 77
Golden Pound Cake, 117
Green Beans, Ortega-Style, 31
Green Chiles
  Avocado and Green Chile Soup, 40
  Caesar Salad with Cilantro and
    Green Chile Dressing, 24
  Corn with Tomatoes and Green
    Chiles, 63
  Fiesta Corn Bread, 66
  Garden-Style Chicken
    Chimichangas, 77
  Green Chile Quesadillas, 94
  Grilled Chicken with Chile Strips
    in Cream, 26
  Marinated Vegetable Salad, 110
  Mexican Taco Salad, 72
  Ortega Apple and Green Chile
    Salad, 58
  Ortega Chile Verde, 67

Green Chiles *continued*
  Ortega Family Green Chile Dip, 51
  Ortega Family Vermicelli, 37
  Ortega Green Chile
    Guacamole, 123
  Ortega Green Chiles with Garlic
    and Oil, 103
  Ortega Ranch-Style Eggs, 44
  Ortega-Style Green Beans, 31
  Shredded Chicken Filling, 109
  Shredded Pork Filling, 109
  Shrimp Tostadas, 90
  Sopes, 26
  Spicy Tomato and Corn Soup, 95
  Spoon Bread with Green Chiles, 63
  Stuffed Chiles in Ranch Sauce, 25
  Tamale Pie, 74
  Tortilla, Green Chile and Lime
    Soup, 40
  White Rice with Green Chiles and
    Tomatoes, 91
  Zucchini with Green Chiles, 110
Grilled Chicken with Chile Strips in
  Cream, 26
Guacamole, Ortega Green Chile, 123

Jalapeño Peppers
  Chilaquiles, 99
  Cinnamon Chocolate Cake, 125
  Fish Veracruz, 41
  Meatloaf Mexicana, 55
  Shredded Beef Filling, 108
  Sopes, 26
  Tamale Pie, 74
  Tostaditas with Fiesta Salsa, 31

Marinated Vegetable Salad, 110
Meatballs in Chile Sauce, 54
Meatless Main Dishes
  Enchilada Stacks, 71
  Ortega Ranch-Style Eggs, 44
  Refried Bean Tostadas, 91
  Spinach and Mushroom
    Enchiladas, 102
  Stuffed Chiles in Ranch Sauce, 25
  Vegetarian Fajitas, 98
Meatloaf Mexicana, 55
Mexicali Corn Salsa, 82
Mexican Hot Chocolate, 111
Mexican Hot Cocoa, 117
Mexican Milk Drink, 45
Mexican Rice, 51
Mexican Taco Salad, 72

Mocha Bread Pudding with Caramel
  Sauce, 113

Original Burrito, The, 87
Original Ortega Tacos, 122
Ortega Family Recipes
  Ortega Apple and Green Chile
    Salad, 58
  Ortega Chicken Fajitas, 50
  Ortega Chile Verde, 67
  Ortega Family Green Chile Dip, 51
  Ortega Family Vermicelli, 37
  Ortega Green Chile Guacamole, 123
  Ortega Green Chiles with Garlic and
    Oil, 103
  Ortega Ranch-Style Eggs, 44
  Ortega-Style Green Beans, 31

Pork
  Chicken and Hominy Soup, 66
  Meatloaf Mexicana, 55
  Ortega Chile Verde, 67
  Shredded Pork Filling, 109
  Tamales, 108
Pudding, Cinnamon Chocolate, 55

Quesadillas
  Fajita Quesadillas, 94
  Green Chile Quesadillas, 94
Quiche, Sausage, 116

Refried Beans
  Burritos Grandes, 87
  Carne Asada Burritos, 86
  Chicken and Bean Burritos, 122
  Creamy Bean Soup, 95
  Enchilada Stacks, 71
  Mexican Taco Salad, 72
  Refried Bean Tostadas, 91
  Shredded Beef with Eggs and
    Tortillas, 45
  Shrimp Tostadas, 90
  Sopes, 26
  Tostaditas with Fiesta Salsa, 31

Rice
  Carne Asada Burritos, 86
  Chicken Mole, 62
  Chicken with Rice, 30
  Meatballs in Chile Sauce, 54
  Mexican Rice, 51
  White Rice with Green Chiles and
    Tomatoes, 91

Salads

Caesar Salad with Cilantro and
 Green Chile Dressing, 24
Marinated Vegetable Salad, 110
Mexican Taco Salad, 72
Ortega Apple and Green Chile
 Salad, 58

Salsa

Avocado and Green Chile Soup, 40
Beef Chimichangas, 58
Burritos Grandes, 87
Carne Asada Burritos, 86
Chicken and Hominy Soup, 66
Chicken Enchiladas with Pickled
 Vegetables, 36
Chicken in Stewed Tomato
 Sauce, 76
Chicken Mole, 62
Chicken with Rice, 30
Chilaquiles, 99
Creamy Bean Soup, 95
Fish Veracruz, 41
Garden-Style Chicken
 Chimichangas, 77
Green Chile Quesadillas, 94
Marinated Vegetable Salad, 110
Meatballs in Chile Sauce, 54
Meatloaf Mexicana, 55
Mexicali Corn Salsa, 82
Mexican Rice, 51
Mexican Taco Salad, 72
Original Burrito, The, 87
Ortega Chicken Fajitas, 50
Ortega Ranch-Style Eggs, 44
Sausage Quiche, 116
Shredded Beef with Eggs and
 Tortillas, 45
Sopes, 26
Spicy Tomato and Corn Soup, 95
Spoon Bread with Green
 Chiles, 63
Stuffed Chiles in Ranch Sauce, 25
Tostaditas with Fiesta Salsa, 31
Vermicelli Soup, 67

Sausage

Cowboy Beans, 59
Sausage Quiche, 116
Shredded Beef Filling, 108
Shredded Beef with Eggs and
 Tortillas, 45
Shredded Chicken Filling, 109
Shredded Pork Filling, 109

Shrimp

Shrimp Enchiladas, 70
Shrimp Tostadas, 90
Sopes, 26

Soups

Avocado and Green Chile Soup, 40
Chicken and Hominy Soup, 66
Creamy Bean Soup, 95
Spicy Tomato and Corn Soup, 95
Tortilla, Green Chile and Lime
 Soup, 40
Vermicelli Soup, 67
Spicy Tomato and Corn Soup, 95
Spinach and Mushroom
 Enchiladas, 102
Spoon Bread with Green Chiles, 63
Stuffed Chiles in Ranch Sauce, 25

Tacos

Baja Fish Tacos, 81
Fajita-Style Beef Soft Tacos, 82
Original Ortega Tacos, 122
Turkey Tacos, 83
Taco Salad, Mexican, 72
Tamale Pie, 74
Tamales, 108
Tortilla, Green Chile and Lime
 Soup, 40

Tortillas (Corn)

Chicken Enchiladas with Pickled
 Vegetables, 36
Chilaquiles, 99
Enchilada Casserole, 71
Enchilada Stacks, 71
Shrimp Enchiladas, 70
Spinach and Mushroom
 Enchiladas, 102

Tortillas (Flour)

Burritos Grandes, 87
Carne Asada Burritos, 86
Chicken and Bean Burritos, 122
Fajita Quesadillas, 94
Fruit-Filled Chimichangas with
 Cinnamon Custard Sauce, 119
Garden-Style Chicken
 Chimichangas, 77
Green Chile Quesadillas, 94
Ortega Chicken Fajitas, 50
Sausage Quiche, 116
Shredded Beef with Eggs and
 Tortillas, 45
Tostaditas with Fiesta Salsa, 31
Vegetarian Fajitas, 98

Tostadas

Refried Bean Tostadas, 91
Shrimp Tostadas, 90
Tostaditas with Fiesta Salsa, 31
Turkey Tacos, 83
Vegetarian Fajitas, 98
Vermicelli Soup, 67

White Rice with Green Chiles and
 Tomatoes, 91

Zucchini with Green Chiles, 110

HISTORICAL NOTES

Chiles, 103
Christmas in Mexico, 111
Cinco de Mayo, 123
Comfort Food, 99
Cooking of El Norte, The, 87
Enchiladas, 71
Flan: The Classic Mexican Dessert, 33
Full of Beans, 59
Golden Egg, The, 44
Making of Posole, The, 66
Meatball Soup, 54
Mexican Holidays, 117
More on Mole, 62
Original Fajita, The 50
Pasta, Mexican Style, 37
Rice: Heart of the Midday Meal, 30
Salsas: Classic to Creative, 82
Shredded Meat, 109
Spanish Influence, The, 41
Stuffing Chiles, 25
Tortillas: Corn vs. Flour, 94
Tostadas, 90
Wedding Cakes, 27

TIPS

Avocados, 123
Buying and Storing Chicken, 62
Buying Mexican Cheese, 116
Buying Shrimp, 90
Chicken Broth Options, 37
Choosing Rice for Mexican
 Cooking, 30
Cooking Fresh Corn, 98
Cooking Fresh Fish, 41
Cornmeal and Corn Flour, 111
Creating Your Own Fajitas, 50
Folding Burritos, 86
Grilling Chicken, 27
Handling Canned Chiles, 24
Preparing Dried Beans, 59
Quick Ortega Chile Ideas, 103
Shaping Meatballs Easily, 54
Taco Buffet, A, 81
Warming Taco Shells, 83

ORTEGA

An early label used on cans of Ortega chiles.

The son of Emigdio and Concepción (Dominguez) Ortega, Emilio C. Ortega was born in Ventura on August 8, 1857. He attended public school, then the Franciscan College, a high school in Santa Barbara, where he graduated in 1873. Following his graduation, he was enrolled at Healds Business College in San Francisco for a year. The whole time he was at school, he yearned to be in the world of business, making a name for himself. His brief college career was followed by a year as a clerk in Samuels' Silk House in San Francisco.

Energized by San Francisco, Emilio returned home to Ventura, 18 years old and full of high hopes and adventure. He talked his father and an uncle into helping him buy a small local grocery store for $35, a business he ran for four years.

Emilio Ortega grew up in the foothills near Ventura, where he later perfected his chile-canning technique.

JOE VIESTI, VIESTI ASSOCIATES, INC.

*"The Gold Rush of Northern California is over, but the
agricultural Gold Rush of Southern California is just
beginning."* — Emilio C. Ortega

But it was difficult for the
ambitious young man to buckle
down under the supervision of a
father and an uncle, especially
since he'd just returned from
Northern California, an area still
bursting with the vitality of the
Gold Rush days. And, despite the
fact that "ventura" is the Spanish
word for "adventure," the small
village was not an exciting place
to live. Emilio's hometown really
hadn't been adventurous since
pirates had claimed it as a hideout
half a century before. So Emilio
sold the store and repaid his
father and uncle, leaving himself
with nothing.

*A gold rush town left from Emilio's
youthful days in Northern California.*

W.P. FLEMING, VIESTI ASSOCIATES, INC.

The New Mexico Years

After working at a variety of
jobs in Central and Southern
California, Emilio moved to New
Mexico in 1890. He became the
general manager and a minor
stockholder of the huge Esmeralds
Rancho in Valencia County. In
1893, he became the assistant
superintendent of the Atlantic
Pacific Railway Company of
Albuquerque, New Mexico.

It was then that Emilio C.
Ortega relaxed and began to truly
enjoy himself. He traded in his fast,
sure-footed ranch horse and bought
himself an elegant horse and
carriage. He became known as a
man about town. Albuquerque
didn't have all the glamour he'd
experienced in San Francisco, but it
did have a lot of great food.

Emilio began dining in
restaurants with friends, following
the tradition of happy eating he'd
experienced while growing up at
home in California. And many
times, after eating a particularly
wonderful dish, he'd ask the cook for
the recipe. He would carefully write
the recipe down, planning to share it
with his family when he returned to
Ventura. In those days, cookbooks
were not as common as they are

today, so travelers often had to jot down different recipes as they came upon them.

It was during these productive years in New Mexico that Emilio made a great discovery. He did not find a place like his great grand-father, José Francisco Ortega, who had found the San Francisco Bay. Instead, Emilio encountered what he thought was one of the greatest and tastiest foods of all time—the famous big, red chile of New Mexico, which had been brought across the border from the great central valley of Mexico nearly a century before.

New Mexicans, who seemed to like the hottest of Mexican foods, loved this chile hot and ripe. But Emilio, being a Californian, preferred this large, long chile when it was in its early stage of development—still green, tender and fairly mild flavored. This also proved to be the best stage for roasting the chile. Even better—after roasting, the chiles could be easily opened, seeded and filled with cheese to make delicious chiles rellenos.

During this exhilarating time in his life Emilio fell ill and had to leave his post with the Atlantic

Pacific Railway Company. He sold his grand horse and carriage and headed back west to California. Besides being ill, Emilio knew his parents were getting older and he wanted to pay them a visit.

Seeds of Opportunity

Back at home, Emilio discovered how easy it was for a son to fall back under the spell of his family, especially at dinnertime when the food was full of rich fragrance and flavor, and the stories were as captivating as ever.

Emilio's father, Emigdio, began telling tales. Emilio realized that no

Emilio loved the chile he tasted in New Mexico, but found he preferred it at a younger stage—when it was still green, tender and mild flavored.

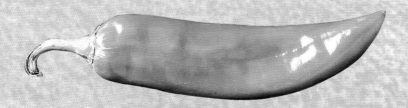

matter how much older he'd grown, his favorite family stories seemed to get better with time.

Joyfully, Emilio told his family how good food and good stories seemed to transcend all barriers and bring people together. He told his mother, Concepción, about the grand chile that he'd found in New Mexico and the salsas the people of that region prepared. He promised to cook up a whole batch of chiles rellenos, New Mexican style, once he regained his strength.

It wasn't long after his homecoming that Emilio, now nearly 36 years old, began to feel stronger and better. After all, good food and good conversation doesn't just feed the stomach, but also the heart and soul.

One morning during the spring of 1894, Emilio came across the seeds of the chiles he'd brought back from New Mexico. He decided to plant some in the garden behind the adobe house. What a surprise! Those New Mexico chiles took to the rich soil and damp climate of Ventura like nobody's business. Emilio had so many chiles the first year that he and his family couldn't eat them all. He began giving them away to friends and other relatives. Everyone loved them!

By the second year's harvest, Emilio's chiles had acclimated quite well to the California coast. For some reason, they grew longer

Emilio Ortega convinced local chile farmers to extend the growing season by planting their chiles two weeks apart. They soon learned he wanted only the biggest and the best.

PETER PURCHIA, VIESTI ASSOCIATES, INC.

Emilio's success was influenced by his father Emigdio and his family, pioneers who settled along the California coast.
Photo courtesy of the Ventura County Museum of History and Art.

and fatter than their New Mexico cousins. Now, everyone really wanted these chiles.

The third year, Emilio hired some extra help and planted a field of chiles just north of his family's adobe, down by the riverbed. He planted only the seeds from his best chiles of the previous year. His efforts paid off. He had so many big chiles ripening, that he couldn't eat or trade them quickly enough. He began giving away baskets of chiles.

A Dream Takes Shape

Emilio was coming to the realization that the climate of California wasn't as dry as the climate of New Mexico, and that once the chiles turned red, they wouldn't keep as long as they did in New Mexico. There, people could actually braid their chiles into long, beautiful arrangements to hang in their kitchens for months. Emilio's green chiles would stay fresh no longer than a week in the California climate.

Emilio began to dream. He was 38 years old, and he had regained his full, vigorous strength.

Ever since he'd had to sell his little grocery store, he'd been working for someone else. But now, before him, were these great chiles and the generous climate of Oxnard and Ventura, just north of the quickly growing metropolis of Los Angeles. Maybe, just maybe, he had the chance of going into business for himself. If there was just some way these delicious chiles could be kept in their tender, green stage before they completely ripened and turned red and too hot, he was sure there was a market for them and maybe even a fortune to be made.

Emilio learned from some local cooks that if the chiles were roasted properly on the comal (cooking surface), then peeled, seeded and washed, they could be stored in jars for some time. But Emilio knew that glass jars broke easily and were far too expensive to be used commercially. Perhaps cans were the answer. He located a business that made cans on 3rd Street in Los Angeles, just beyond the mountains. Acquiring some cans, Emilio began to tinker around in his family's little adobe.

He wanted to find a way to roast and can these chiles he'd brought from New Mexico. He knew if he could just make it possible for people to enjoy the taste of these green chiles year-round, he could make history.

So Emilio went to work on his chile-preservation idea with a passion, rolling up his sleeves right in his parents' adobe kitchen. But, as so often happens with dreams,

what he got was not necessarily what he was looking for. Emilio had been at work for only a few weeks when he discovered it was far easier to can salsa than to preserve whole green chiles. In fact, the larger and meatier the chiles were, the harder it was to get the stubborn things to lie flat in a container.

A seemingly unconnected event eventually solved Emilio's problem. This just happened to be the year that he helped his father replace the rafters of their little adobe home. The two men took a cart and horse to salvage the rafters from the broken-down buildings around the old mission. Emilio was amazed at the workmanship that had gone into the rafters nearly 70 years before. It was of such high quality that the wood could be used again to repair their adobe.

HOWARD MILLARD, VIESTI ASSOCIATES, INC.

Emilio Ortega had seen New Mexican cooks thread their red chiles on ropes to store for months, but he knew his tender green chiles would not stay fresh that long. He resolved to find another way. Canning was his ultimate answer.

To Ortega, green chiles were as important to good Mexican cooking as the tortilla.

JOE VIESTI, VIESTI ASSOCIATES, INC.

Near the rafters, Emilio noticed some scrap iron and tossed it into the wagon along with the wood. He didn't know how yet, but he had an idea that the iron might be helpful in his quest to can chiles.

He was still determined to find a way to roast and can the chiles. They had to be the most delicious vegetable he'd ever eaten. In fact, he was sure they had been partly responsible for his recovery.

That winter, Emilio tinkered over the open fire in his mother's kitchen with the deep, rounded piece of iron he'd brought from the mission. Eventually, he figured out that if he added a top to the piece of iron, making it into a cylinder-like pan, he could then roll the chiles flat by hand. This was an enormous breakthrough.

With this rolling cylinder, Emilio now found that one person working the roller could actually do more than 12 cooks working with forks, roasting the chiles on the comal. Also, when the chiles were rolled this way, part of their skins came off, too. They seemed to get softer and more manageable, especially after they were seeded and washed.

That next chile season, in late August 1897, Emilio canned his first whole green chiles using his new roller, and a big batch of salsa.

The seemingly unattainable miracle of having year-round, green, tender chiles had become a reality. The concept of having chiles on the shelf, just sitting there ready for slipping into a

cheese quesadilla, or for making chiles rellenos—previously one of the most difficult and time-consuming of Mexican dishes—was now easy, really easy.

Ortega Chile Company

Late that same year, in 1897, Emilio founded the Pioneer Ortega Chile Packing Company, the first commercial food operation in the state of California. In keeping with the pioneering spirit of his ancestors,

An Ortega chile can from 1910.

BACKGROUND PHOTO: JOE VIESTI VIESTI ASSOCIATES, INC.

> *"Residents of today, surrounded by commodities of today, have no idea of the hardships suffered by our predecessors when they built a home or a business."* — Emilio C. Ortega

Emilio worked long into the night, day after day, with only a relative or two helping him, trying to keep up with the huge crop and the increasing demand. Everyone wanted his chiles.

It was during this time that Emilio first shared his great vision with his family. He told them that he saw his company's product as a special helper to every home cook, and a second pair of hands to every restaurant chef. The possibilities were limitless! And, Emilio wasn't going to be satisfied until he'd introduced this chile to the rest of the world.

That year, word of Emilio's dream and his chiles spread as far as Los Angeles, and even down to Anaheim, California. Farmers wanted to purchase seeds from him. Emilio began to see that he was going to have to borrow big money, maybe even $1,000, and move his brand-new packing company to Los Angeles. He would take his best seeds with him and recruit local farmers to grow the chiles for him. Also, the cans he was using were manufactured in Los Angeles, and he wanted to be closer to that source.

This was going to be a big gamble, the biggest he'd ever taken. He knew that, with one early frost or big rain, he could lose everything.

Los Angeles Bound

It was now 1899; Emilio was 42 years old, and he was full of big plans. Coming home in poor health had been a blessing in disguise. His recuperation time had given him the chance to rest and

Home to Emilio's family for more than 40 years, the Ortega adobe marks the birthplace of the Ortega Chile Company. Built in 1857 by Emilio's father Emigdio, the adobe still stands today as a testament to the family's many accomplishments.
Photo courtesy of the Ventura County Museum of History and Art.

reorganize within the structure of his family—a place of warmth, trust and love. It had provided him with good, robust, real food for the mind, body and soul.

When Emilio C. Ortega came over the coastal mountains from Ventura to Los Angeles with his

ORTEGA

Early company letters were sent on Ortega's brightly colored stationery.

chiles and grand ideas, he found a bustling city awaiting him, bursting with vibrant energy and high hopes, just like himself. They were a perfect match.

After borrowing money, Emilio set up his plant at 811 Stephens Avenue. Olvera Street, the oldest street in Los Angeles today, was a few blocks away, just across from the railroad station.

That year, with a much improved hand-rolling roaster, Emilio was able to package more than 1,000 cans of whole chiles and about 3,000 cans of salsa. And he discovered two facts during his first year of production: One—the chiles came in from the fields too fast for him to handle; and two—the demand for his chiles, once people tasted them, was far greater than he'd ever dreamed.

Emilio was experiencing first-hand what great men and women have been discovering since the birth of time—that in dreams there is greatness, and in passion there is power. His dreams were coming true, but not without taking some risks.

So the following year, in 1900, Emilio borrowed more money and put himself deeper into debt. He

asked the farmers in Anaheim, where the soil and climate were much like Ventura, to plant their crops two weeks apart. He was hoping that, in this way, he could expand the season of the green chile, not just from the last part of August to the last part of September, but from early August all the way into October—an unheard-of feat.

A Longer Chile Season

At first, many of the farmers balked at Emilio's suggestion, saying that they knew farming and they were not going to fight against the natural seasons and Mother Nature. It was only due to Emilio's conviction and commanding presence that he was able to convince a couple of farmers that if they stuck with him, there was a great future for them in this land of opportunity.

"The Gold Rush of Northern California is over," Emilio was heard to say time and again, "but the agricultural Gold Rush of Southern California is just beginning!"

Inspired by Emilio's words, the farmers in Anaheim grew so many chiles for the Pioneer Ortega

Chile Company over the next 40 years that the name "Anaheim Chile" became synonymous with Ortega, and the chile is still referred to in this way today. But, in truth, the Anaheim Chile, which is also called the Santa Ana Chile, came from the original seeds that Emilio brought back from New Mexico.

That year, by staggering the crops every two weeks, Emilio was able to extend his chile-canning season from 40 to almost 90 days. This was the beginning of the legend of Emilio's genius and resourcefulness.

By his third year in Los Angeles, Emilio was being approached by droves of farmers who wanted to plant crops for him in any way that he suggested.

Emilio started telling the farmers that it wasn't enough for them to just stagger the crops for him. They'd also have to go through their fields early in the season and thin out their plants, because from now on, he would only take the largest and juiciest of chiles. He was not in the business

ORTEGA

A paperweight commemorating Ortega's Green Chile Salsa.

12

At the early Ortega plant, green chiles were received fresh from the growers, then placed in huge hoppers for thorough cleaning.

ORTEGA

of just acquiring chiles, but of accepting only the finest. When people in a grocery store reached for the cans bearing his name, Ortega wanted them to know they were getting only the best.

In 1905, Emilio bought a lot at the corner of 6th and Santa Fe. His business was growing so quickly that he managed to pay off his first loan and establish a longer-range note with the bank in a matter of six years.

By 1910, just as the Mexican Revolution was brewing across the border, Emilio had more than 75 people working for him during the height of the chile season and a dozen people working for him year-round.

The chile-canning season stretched from August until the

first part of November, or until the first rains or big frosts hit. The canning of the salsa, on the other hand, could continue through November and into the first part of December.

The Growing Company

By the mid 1920s, Ortega had doubled his workforce. He had more than 200 people working for him during the height of the chile season and at least 50 people during the longer season of making salsa.

Emilio, who had always been tall and well dressed, was now never seen without a vest and a suit, even when he went out to the fields to inspect the rows of chiles to see if they were good enough to bear the Ortega label.

This was not a job that Emilio took lightly, for he remembered the 70-year-old rafters from the old mission and understood the importance of quality. Emilio and his company were a fine example that the secret to the success of any endeavor was quality work and a keen eye for detail.

Emilio C. Ortega's chiles had become synonymous with Mexican food. And Mexican cuisine had become the rage in the United States. Hot, spicy food was as Californian as sitting under a palm tree enjoying the good life.

Emilio's personal life was also flourishing. In 1925, at the age of 68, Emilio fell in love with a beautiful, young Mexican girl with light brown hair and large hazel eyes. He was almost 40 years her

13

"The secret to the success of any endeavor is quality work and a keen eye to detail." — Emilio C. Ortega

GENUINE
SPANISH
SAUCE

ORTEGA'S
SALSA

RED CHILE SALSA
NET CONTENTS 10 OZS.

PREPARED AND PACKED BY
E. C. Ortega Co. Inc.
LOS ANGELES · CALIFORNIA

An early can of Ortega's red chile salsa.

senior and most men his age were thinking of retiring, but he knew he didn't want to live without her. Mary Magdeline Bustemante and Emilio C. Ortega were married later that same year, and life was adventurous and fulfilling.

One year later, Emilio was the proud father of his first daughter, Emily, a bundle of energy with the biggest, brightest eyes he'd ever seen. Two years later, he and Mary were the happy parents of Evelyn.

Mary and Emilio were the talk of the town, not because of their age difference, but because of the great love they shared.

The founder of the Ortega chile had become a legend. Throughout the 1930s, Emilio continued to walk the fields during the summer months. He

Once cleaned, the chiles were carried by conveyor belt to one of the many busy peeling rooms at the Ortega plant.

ORTEGA

would watch the dark green chile plants grow from finger-size buds into knee-high, robust plants. Often, Emilio took his older daughter, Emily, on these field trips, in an effort to share with her what he knew about the chile business. Upon returning home, he would whip off his suit jacket, put on an apron over his shirt and vest, and go straight to work in the kitchen, cooking up a batch of chiles rellenos or quesadillas, and regaling his daughter with stories of days gone by. These were wonderful days for Emily, helping her father in the kitchen and learning the love and the art of great food and great conversation.

Emilio was now in his 80s, the founder of one of the most steadily growing companies in Los Angeles, and he had a wonderful wife and two beautiful little daughters who loved him. He was still a man as strong as iron and a true believer in good food. He also believed in the integrity of clean, safe facilities for his workers. In fact, some of Emilio's workers, who'd started in his first location in Los Angeles, were still with him after 30 years. Emilio saw these people as family, a connection to his roots that brought him great personal pride.

With the start of World War II in Europe, all of Southern California was transformed overnight. Good food—real food with substance—was needed to feed the hungry giant of the United States, a nation that hadn't tapped its full potential yet.

Southern California continued to blossom into the greatest agricultural center the world had seen since the time of the great Nile and ancient Egypt.

It was during this time, in 1942, when Emily was 14 and Evelyn 12, that Emilio passed away. He was 84 years old and still full of dreams and high hopes. He is remembered as a man who'd always understood the basics of life—family, food, trust and love.

Modern Times

World War II brought a global consciousness to every man and woman on the street. After the war, a new sense of fate and grandeur existed in Southern California. In the middle of this exciting time, the Ortega

BACKGROUND PHOTO: MARK DOWNEY, VIESTI ASSOCIATES, INC.

new tasty

Ortega
brands

Ortega
brands
recipes

ORTEGA

Early recipe books and press coverage were two reasons the Ortega name came to stand for authentic Mexican foods that bring families together.

Company grew faster than ever, for rooted in its very strong foundation had been a man with vision and integrity.

In 1946, the new owners of the Ortega Chile Company moved their plant to Oxnard, California, just across the river from Ventura of all places, where Emilio C. Ortega had started his dream in his parents' adobe.

The stories of Emilio carrying buckets of water by hand from the river to his family's adobe to wash his chiles were now viewed as folklore, like other great legends of American heroes.

Now the acres that farmers were commissioned to farm for Ortega numbered in the thousands. The tractor replaced the horse, and entire new systems of irrigation took over from the buckets of Emilio's day. But, due to the genius of Emilio C. Ortega, the Ortega Company still controlled the chile seeds. It continued to improve upon the seeds by hiring agriculture students from the University of California who knew how to breed plants to select the best characteristics.

ORTEGA

Workers line up outside the Ortega Packing Plant.

rnia Romance
ritten Into the Packing of Spanish Foods

By LLOYD L. STAGGERS

n Joaquin | of which serve a different commercial | lation of seed. Meanwhile, the Royal | That was a score of years ago. Today,
g a reputa- | purpose. | Packing Co., another pioneer chili | California and not Spain sets the
bold bad | Next the cans are filled. Lightly | packer, was anxious to add pimientos | standard by which canned pimientos
repared chili | sealed, they spend approximately 13 | to its line. | are judged.
ile but effec- | minutes in a steam heated exhaust | | Except for a rather limited quantity
were seared | box, after which a "double seamer" | **Start Was Interesting** | produced in Georgia, the pimiento can-
silitate peeling | completes the can-sealing process. | Embargos are not always effective | ning industry of the United States is
years ago, a | Without the delay of a split second, | and in 1910 or thereabout, a thimbleful | centered in Southern California.
spanish lineage | they pass on into a rotary cooker. The | of seed from Calhorra, Spain reached | It is likewise interesting to learn
doing mechani- | trip through this steam-heated box | Los Angeles. C. E. Utt of Tustin un- | that despite unsettled economics, the
senoras did by | varies with the condition of the prod- | dertook the task of producing a crop | producers of chilis and pimientos in
ea was built an | uct, but averages about 23 minutes. | from this meager supply of seed. No | Southern California have consistently
| | royal heir ever received greater care | profited from their labors. They have
Ortega. Today, | Continuing the journey, the cans are | than did the little plot in which it was | made a little money from their crops
is still vitally in- | cooled, counted and carried to a desig- | planted. The experiment was a suc- | right through the depression. In fact,
many which bears | nated part of the plant for storage, by | cess. Seed enough to plant five acres | when the chili growers petitioned the
| means of gravity conveyors. Running | was obtained. Thus the entire pimiento | farm relief organization for a code,
| as capacity and utilizing several "lines" | industry of California is founded on | some months ago, the authorities at
| to capacity and utilizing several "lines" | that one thimble full of seed that left | Washington sent back a report that
nique in many re- | minute pass through the sealing and | Spain unheralded and without the | they were not in need of financial aid
y two businesses in | cooking machinery. Obviously, this | benefit of passport. | and that no code would be forthcom-
similar, but distinct | work is largely automatic. | With neither knowledge or preced- | ing.
d: chilis and pimien- | | ent for guidance, the initial canning | E. C. Ortega Co. and Royal Pack-
only about 90 days a | Pimientos—"sweet peppers"—are | operations were both crude and costly. | ing Co. now operate as a related or-
at over 5,000,000 cans | handled in much the same way, and | New York buyers laughed with deri- | ganization, of which C. J. "Tex" Wal-
cento products. All of | several varieties of peppers are canned, | sion when they cut the first samples. | den is the presiding genius.
inery in the plant was | along with special products of a re- | |
ned by its own engi- | lated nature. Chilis are packed in 4 | |
in its own workshop. | oz. and No. 2½ cans. Pimientos come | |
Tex Walden escorted | in two additional sizes: 7¼ and 15 | |
se plant the other day, it | ounce. | |
t round-up of the chili | | |
n. | **Has History** | |
| In storage, the cans are stacked un- | |
vn chiefly in Los Angeles | labeled, according to variety. Not a | |
counties, come to the | can receives a label until it has stood | |
ng platform in sacks. By | for at least 20 days. This permits all | |
al conveyor, they are car- | swells to be eliminated before the | |
rting platform, where they | goods are cased, thereby doing away | |
ir initial inspection. Pep- | with that bugaboo of the canning | |
for use are discarded and | trade, the "swell allowance." | |
pass on to the roasters. | As the Fire Chief "sticks to his | |
briefly, these roasters are | horse," the Ortega plant continues to | |
l cylinders or drums, heated | operate by steam, even in this day of | |
degrees, Fahrenheit, through | multifarious electrification and motori- | |
ne peppers pass. In a three- | zation. Steam has proven both effi- | |
journey, the skins are seared | cient and economical. Two 125 horse | |
sened, without cooking the fruit | power boilers, oil-fired and automati- | |
at term can be applied to such | cally controlled, furnish steam for the | |
ric product of the soil. In a | cookers and exhaust boxes. Having | |
washer, a heavy spray of water | performed that necessary function, the | |
r loosens the peel and cools the | steam passes on through an engine | |
ed peppers. | which drives the machinery. | |
| Development of the pimiento can- | |
ble conveyors deliver | ning industry in Southern California | |
ove the | is in itself an absorbing story. Not | |
| r many years, Spain had a virtual | |

Machinery like that found in no other plant aids deft-fingered girls in the work of packing chilis, pimientos and other "Spanish" products in the efficient factory of E. C. Ortega Co.

The processing and packing of Ortega chiles and salsas followed modern methods as a result of Ortega's experiments in the early stages of the industry.

In the Ortega processing plants, modernization also replaced some of the steps formerly done by hand. Automated roasters were now used at the Oxnard facility, fed by conveyer belts that were powered with huge diesel engines. These roasters were four feet around and 20 feet long, with steps inside to keep the chiles flipping while a great flame shot through the center of the roaster.

Now 400 to 500 people worked on each shift, with two shifts running per day during the height of the chile season. The season, of course, had been extended through the genius of Emilio, by staggering the planting of the crops.

By the 1960s, Ortega brand chiles and salsa were the biggest sellers in all 11 Western states, but there was still room to grow. At this time, a man who would later become known as "Mr. Chile" was hired by Ortega. He was wooed from one of the largest food companies on the East Coast, where he'd been a plant manager for more than 20 years.

From 1966 to 1985, Mr. Chile helped take Ortega from three slow-turning roasters to huge, flame-shooting, fast-rolling ones. By 1985, the company had 30 mammoth roasters, producing 7 million 4-ounce cans of chiles, 2.5 million 7-ounce cans, and 75,000 cases of the 2.5-pound cans.

Another change was made possible through the work of a brilliant young botanist. He improved the Ortega chile by developing a hybrid that had three veins instead of two. The three-veined chiles could be flattened on the conveyer belt, making it easier for the workers to cut out the veins and seeds.

Employees Remember

Numbers give an impressive overall view of the company's steady growth, but it is through the eyes of loyal workers that one can truly understand the effects of Ortega's modernization. Many things have changed, but many traditions remain.

The men and women who've worked on the packing lines for more than 30 years reflect on what they've seen in the plant. These stories are typical.

One woman, who came from Mexico in the late 1950s, started working in the fields cutting Ortega chiles. A year later, she earned a job in the plant as one of the hundreds of workers who would clean the chiles. She would pluck the chiles from the conveyer belt, cut off the tops, take out the seeds, devein them, and put them into a pan. After she filled the pan, another worker would put it on the next conveyer belt to take the chiles to the washers.

In her third year of working at the plant, a new machine meant the workers no longer had to cut off the tops. Instead, they just lined up the chiles carefully, so the machine could cut off the tops.

Emilio Ortega (right) at his cousin's ranch.

Emilio Ortega (right) at his cousin's ranch.
Photo courtesy of the Ventura County Museum of History and Art.

Cartons of Ortega chiles sit ready for shipping around the world.

Another 30-year veteran from the plant showed how she used to pack the cans. She would pick up four big chiles with her right hand and put them in her left hand. Then, pointing the tips toward her, she would lower them into the can on the side nearest her, then roll the flattened chiles into the back side of the can. "So the chiles can rest," she said, "quietly and peacefully, looking so fat and delicious." This tradition of hand packing whole chiles still remains. Today the chiles are still inspected by people who know how to ensure the kind of quality that Emilio himself had come to expect.

A Century of Ortega

In 1995, Nestlé purchased the Ortega brand. Nestlé believed in

"When shoppers reach for Ortega chiles, I want them to know they're getting the best." — Emilio C. Ortega

An old can label for Ortega's green chile salsa. Notice the illustration of the Ortega family adobe in the middle. The chile-ringed adobe was the Ortega trademark that appeared on many early Ortega labels.

the integrity of Emilio Ortega and the high quality of his chiles. How else could the Ortega company have survived for 100 years?

Nestlé is in the food market for one reason. The company has never bought or produced "products." Instead Nestlé buys and produces "brands." Products may come and go, but when a company buys a brand, it is making a commitment. It is guaranteeing the brand will maintain its character and quality, and that it will be sustained long into the future.

With a brand like Ortega, Nestlé is making a promise. So today, when a family picks up a can of Ortega chiles or salsa from the supermarket shelf, they know they are getting the best, just as shoppers did in the days of Emilio C. Ortega. It's that kind of reputation that would have made Emilio smile—the penchant for quality that makes Ortega proud to celebrate 100 years of canning the best chiles around.

©Victor E. Villaseñor, 1997

Emilio C. Ortega with his wife Mary and daughters Emily and Evelyn.
Photo courtesy of the Ventura County Museum of History and Art.

19

A Century
of Ortega

Grilled Chicken with Chile Strips in Cream (front right) (recipe page 26);
Caesar Salad with Cilantro and Green Chile Dressing (back right) (recipe page 24);
Sopes (front left) (recipe page 26)

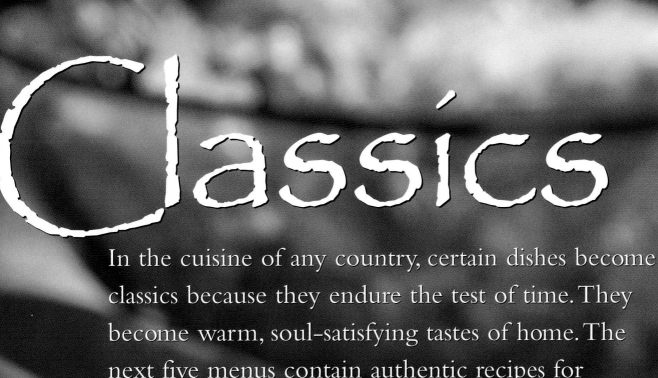

Classics

In the cuisine of any country, certain dishes become classics because they endure the test of time. They become warm, soul-satisfying tastes of home. The next five menus contain authentic recipes for Mexican classics such as chiles rellenos, fideo, huevos rancheros and creamy custard flan. Prepare these classics for your family and make them a tradition in your home.

At the heart of every Mexican gathering is fabulous food.

Lavish meals are the order of the day for friends

and family. Serve this sumptuous menu to your guests for a taste

of authentic Mexican hospitality.

A Yucatán Feast

Sopes

Grilled Chicken with Chile Strips in Cream
~ *or* ~
Stuffed Chiles in Ranch Sauce

Oven-roasted New Potatoes

Ortega Refried Beans with Shredded Cheese

Caesar Salad with Cilantro and Green Chile Dressing

Chocolate Chip Mexican Wedding Cakes

Cinnamon-Flavored Coffee

Stuffed Chiles in Ranch Sauce
(recipe page 25)

Caesar Salad with Cilantro and Green Chile Dressing

ENSALADA CESAR CON ADEREZO DE CILANTRO Y CHILES VERDES

Green chiles, pumpkin seeds and cilantro add a unique twist to the dressing for this classic salad. Caesar salad is said to have been created by Tijuana chef Caesar Cardini at the turn of the century.

Cilantro and Green Chile Dressing
    1 cup (about 1 bunch) fresh cilantro leaves
    ¾ cup mayonnaise
    ¾ cup vegetable oil
    ½ cup (4-ounce can) ORTEGA Diced Green Chiles
    ¼ cup red wine vinegar
    ¼ cup pumpkin seeds (pepitas), toasted
    ¼ cup (1 ounce) crumbled cotija or feta cheese
    1 clove garlic, peeled
    ½ teaspoon salt
    ⅛ teaspoon ground black pepper

Caesar Salad
    1 large head romaine lettuce, rinsed, patted dry and chopped
    2 cups seasoned croutons
    ½ cup (4-ounce can) ORTEGA Whole Green Chiles, cut into strips
    ½ cup (2 ounces) crumbled cotija or feta cheese
    ½ cup pumpkin seeds (pepitas), toasted

For Cilantro and Green Chile Dressing:
PLACE cilantro, mayonnaise, oil, chiles, vinegar, pumpkin seeds, cheese, garlic, salt and pepper in food processor or blender container; cover. Process until coarsely chopped. Cover; chill for 1 hour or until flavors are blended.

For Caesar Salad:
COMBINE lettuce, croutons, chiles, cheese and pumpkin seeds in large bowl. Add ½ cup Cilantro and Green Chile Dressing; toss well to coat. Store unused dressing in refrigerator for up to one week. Makes 8 servings.

Handling Canned Chiles

The membranes of a chile are its hottest part. Because the membranes have already been taken out of canned chiles, they do not contain the burning oils that make fresh chiles more difficult to use.

How you handle canned chiles depends on how you intend to use them. Whole chiles intended for stuffing (as for chiles rellenos) should be drained and laid out on a flat surface before filling. They may also be drained, sliced and added to salads as in the above recipe. Diced, canned chiles can simply be drained and added to your favorite recipe.

Stuffed Chiles in Ranch Sauce

CHILES RELLENOS EN SALSA RANCHERA

Be sure the oil for frying these cheese-stuffed peppers is hot enough to ensure a crisp, golden coating. To test, drop in some batter to see if it quickly rises to the surface.

Ranch Sauce
- 1 tablespoon vegetable oil
- 1 cup (1 small) chopped onion
- 1 cup (1 small) chopped red, green and/or yellow bell pepper
- 1 clove garlic, finely chopped
- 2½ cups (24-ounce jar) ORTEGA Thick & Chunky Salsa, mild
- ½ cup water
- 1 MAGGI Chicken Bouillon Cube
- 2 bay leaves
- 1 cinnamon stick, broken into pieces
- ½ teaspoon dried oregano, crushed

Stuffed Chiles
- 2 cans (7 ounces *each*) ORTEGA Whole Green Chiles
- 8 ounces Monterey Jack cheese, cut into 1 x 2-inch strips
- 3 eggs, separated
- 3 tablespoons all-purpose flour
- Vegetable oil

For Ranch Sauce:

HEAT oil in large saucepan over medium-high heat. Add onion, bell pepper and garlic; cook, stirring constantly, for 1 to 2 minutes or until onion is tender. Stir in salsa, water, bouillon, bay leaves, cinnamon and oregano. Bring to a boil. Reduce heat to low; cook for 10 to 15 minutes or until flavors are blended. Remove bay leaves and cinnamon pieces.

For Stuffed Chiles:

STUFF each chile (being careful not to break skins) with cheese. Beat egg whites in small mixer bowl until stiff peaks form. Whisk egg yolks in small bowl until creamy. Fold egg yolks and flour into egg whites until just combined.

ADD oil to 1-inch depth in medium skillet; heat over high heat for 3 to 4 minutes. Dip chiles in batter until well coated. Place in oil; fry, turning frequently with tongs, until golden brown. Remove from skillet; place on paper towels to soak. Serve stuffed chiles warm with Ranch Sauce. Makes 5 servings.

Stuffing Chiles

In this country, the mild poblano pepper is most familiar to fans of chiles rellenos. It is about the same size as a green bell pepper, only longer and more slender.

In pepper-loving Mexico, though, any pepper that is able to hold a filling is stuffed—even dried peppers such as the smoky pasilla or pasado.

In Veracruz, fiery jalapeños are stuffed with meat, then batter fried. In other regions of Mexico, peppers are stuffed with cheeses, mixtures of chorizo and potatoes or shredded crab or shrimp. One version of chiles rellenos—the essence of simplicity— calls for a pepper to be stuffed with warmed refried beans, then eaten unbattered. The recipe in this book calls for Ortega chiles to be stuffed with cheese before batter frying.

Sopes

Serve these crisp, savory cakes as appetizers at your next party. Guests will love topping them with beans, cheese, salsa, Ortega Pickled Jalapeño Slices and sour cream.

  2 cups masa harina flour (Mexican corn masa mix)
  ¼ cup shortening or lard
1¼ cups warm water
  ½ cup (4-ounce can) ORTEGA Diced Green Chiles
  3 teaspoons vegetable oil, *divided*
1¾ cups (1-pound can) ORTEGA Refried Beans, warmed
  1 cup (4 ounces) shredded cheddar or Monterey Jack cheese or crumbled cotija
      cheese (optional)
    Sour cream (optional)
    ORTEGA Thick & Chunky Salsa, mild (optional)
    ORTEGA Pickled Jalapeño Slices (optional)

PLACE flour in large bowl; cut in shortening with pastry blender or two knives until mixture resembles coarse crumbs. Gradually add water, kneading dough until smooth. Add chiles; mix well. Form dough into 16 small balls. Pat each ball into 3-inch patty; place on waxed paper.

HEAT *1 teaspoon* oil in large skillet over medium-high heat for 1 to 2 minutes. Cook patties for 3 minutes on each side or until golden brown, adding some of the *remaining* oil as needed to prevent sticking.

TOP with beans, cheese, sour cream, salsa and pickled jalapeño slices. Makes 16 appetizer servings.

Grilled Chicken with Chile Strips in Cream

POLLO A LA PARRILLA CON RAJAS EN CREMA

Chile peppers are tossed in a creamy cheese sauce to make a delightful topping for chicken.

  2 tablespoons vegetable oil
  1 cup (1 small) chopped onion
  2 tablespoons all-purpose flour
1½ cups milk
  1 package (3 ounces) cream cheese, cut into pieces
  ½ teaspoon garlic salt
  2 cans (7 ounces *each*) ORTEGA Whole Green Chiles, drained, rinsed
      and cut into strips
  6 boneless, skinless chicken breast halves, grilled (see tip next page)
    Chopped fresh parsley

HEAT oil in large skillet over medium-high heat. Add onion; cook, stirring occasionally, for 1 to 2 minutes or until onion is tender. Sprinkle flour over onion; cook, stirring constantly, for 1 to 2 minutes or until flour is golden brown.

ADD milk slowly to skillet; bring to a boil. Cook, stirring constantly, for 3 to 4 minutes or until mixture is thickened. Reduce heat to low. Add cream cheese and garlic salt. Cook for 2 to 3 minutes or until cream cheese is melted and combined. Stir in chiles; heat through. Top chicken breasts with chiles in cream. Sprinkle with parsley. Makes 6 servings.

Chocolate Chip Mexican Wedding Cakes

Chocolate and cinnamon—two favorite flavors of Mexico—add new twists to these traditional cookies.

> 1 cup (2 sticks) butter, softened
> ½ cup sifted powdered sugar
> 1 teaspoon vanilla extract
> 2 cups all-purpose flour
> ⅔ cup finely chopped nuts
> 2 to 2½ teaspoons ground cinnamon
> 2 cups (12-ounce package) NESTLÉ TOLL HOUSE Semi-Sweet
>   Chocolate Morsels, *divided*

BEAT butter and powdered sugar in large mixer bowl until creamy. Beat in vanilla. Gradually beat in flour, nuts and cinnamon. Stir in *1½ cups* morsels. Roll dough into 1-inch balls; place on ungreased baking sheets.

BAKE in preheated 350°F. oven for 10 to 12 minutes or until set and light golden brown on bottom. Cool for 2 minutes on baking sheets; remove to wire racks to cool completely.

MICROWAVE *remaining* morsels in heavy-duty plastic bag on HIGH (100%) power for 30 seconds; knead. Microwave at additional 10- to 20-second intervals, kneading until smooth. Cut tiny corner from bag; squeeze to drizzle over cookies. Chill cookies for about 5 minutes or until chocolate is set. Store at room temperature in airtight containers. Makes about 4½ dozen cookies.

Wedding Cakes

Despite their name, these luscious "cakes" are really cookies. "Cookie" is simply the English derivative of a Dutch word meaning "little cake." South of the border, these round cookies are often rolled in powdered sugar and wrapped in white tissue paper, like a bridal veil. The ends of the paper are twisted so they look like bonbons. For the best flavor and texture, be sure to use butter—not margarine.

Grilling Chicken

In Mexico there is a long tradition of cooking a variety of meats over coals in an outdoor barbecue pit or grill.

In fact, phrases referring to grilling tools are found throughout the Spanish language, as are words for the cooking method's delicious end result. Pollo a las brasas means "chicken over the embers" and barbacoa de pollo means pit-barbecued or grilled chicken. The meat is often flavored with mesquite wood or banana or avocado leaves that Mexican cooks add to the coals. You may not have avocado or banana leaves on hand, but you'll find grilled chicken dishes (like the one on the previous page) are always popular. To grill chicken, remember these guidelines:

A half-chicken weighing between 1¼ and 1½ pounds will take 40 to 50 minutes over medium coals; a 4- to 5-ounce boneless, skinless chicken breast half will take 12 to 15 minutes over medium coals; and bone-in meaty chicken pieces or chicken quarters weighing between 2 and 2½ pounds total will take 35 to 50 minutes over medium coals.

Place the chicken pieces directly on the grill over the preheated coals. Grill, uncovered, until the meat is tender and no longer pink in the center or near the bone. Be sure to turn the chicken halfway through the grilling time.

In days past, Sunday dinner wasn't complete

without well-seasoned chicken slowly cooked to tender perfection.

Recreate this time-honored tradition with this classic Mexican menu

featuring "Arroz con Pollo"—chicken with rice.

Classic Chicken Dinner

Tostaditas with Fiesta Salsa

Chicken with Rice

Ortega-Style Green Beans

Dinner Rolls

Cream Cheese Flan

Coffee and Tea

Chicken with Rice
Ortega-Style Green Beans
(recipes pages 30 and 31)

Chicken with Rice

Arroz con Pollo

In many Mexican households, rice flavored with any combination of broth, tomatoes, chiles and cheese constitutes a full meal. This classic dish—featuring flavorful rice and chicken—is one well-known example.

    4 **slices bacon**
1½ **pounds chicken parts**
    1 **cup (1 small) chopped onion**
    1 **cup (1 large) chopped green bell pepper**
    2 **large cloves garlic, finely chopped**
    2 **cups long-grain white rice**
2½ **cups (24-ounce jar) ORTEGA Thick & Chunky Salsa, mild**
1¾ **cups (14½-ounce can) chicken broth**
    1 **cup (8-ounce can) CONTADINA Dalla Casa Buitoni Tomato Sauce**
    1 **teaspoon salt**
  ½ **teaspoon ground cumin**
     Chopped fresh parsley

COOK bacon in large saucepan with lid over medium-high heat until crispy; remove from saucepan. Crumble bacon; set aside. Add chicken to saucepan; cook, turning frequently, for 5 to 7 minutes or until browned on all sides. Remove from saucepan. Discard all but *2 tablespoons* drippings from saucepan.

ADD onion, bell pepper and garlic; cook, stirring occasionally, for 3 to 4 minutes or until crisp-tender. Add rice; cook for 2 to 3 minutes. Stir in salsa, broth, tomato sauce, salt and cumin. Bring to a boil; place chicken over rice mixture. Reduce heat to low; cover. Cook for 20 to 25 minutes or until most of moisture is absorbed and chicken is no longer pink near bone. Sprinkle with bacon and parsley. Makes 6 servings.

Choosing Rice for Mexican Cooking

When a Mexican dish calls for rice, use long-grain rice. This popular rice got its name by being about four to five times as long as it is wide. The cooked grains are light and fluffy and tend to remain separate— even while being stored.

To save time on future meals, cook extra rice. Simply store cooked rice in an airtight container in the refrigerator for up to 1 week or in the freezer for up to 6 months.

To reheat chilled or frozen rice, place it in a saucepan with 2 tablespoons liquid (water or broth) for each cup of rice. Cover; heat over low heat for 5 minutes or until the rice is heated through.

Rice: Heart of the Midday Meal

Rice, which was introduced to Mexico by the Spaniards, has become a standard of the comida—the traditional midday meal. The comida's five courses comprise a New World interpretation of European eating patterns.

For the comida, the first dish is a bowl of soup, most often made with a chicken broth. That is followed by a rice dish (called a "dry soup" because of its flavorings), a meat dish, a bowl of beans and dessert.

Morisqueta refers to plain boiled rice seasoned only with a pinch of sea salt. In Mexico, morisqueta is considered comfort food for sick days, rainy days or any day.

Tostaditas with Fiesta Salsa
TOSTADITAS CON SALSA FIESTA

Traditionally, tostaditas are made by frying tortilla wedges. This baked version yields crisp, golden chips without frying.

- **4 (8-inch) soft taco–size flour tortillas, cut into quarters**
- **1¾ cups (1-pound can) ORTEGA Refried Beans, warmed**
- **1½ cups (6 ounces) shredded cheddar or Monterey Jack cheese or crumbled queso fresco**
- **Fiesta Salsa (recipe follows)**
- **Additional Topping Suggestions: sliced avocados, ORTEGA Green Chile Guacamole (recipe page 123), sour cream, ORTEGA Pickled Jalapeño Slices, shredded lettuce, chopped tomatoes, sliced ripe olives and chopped fresh cilantro**

PLACE tortilla triangles on greased baking sheets. Bake in preheated 450°F. oven for 3 to 4 minutes or until slightly golden and crisp. Remove from oven.

SPREAD 1 to 1½ tablespoons beans over each triangle; sprinkle with 2 teaspoons cheese. Return to oven; bake for additional 1 to 2 minutes or until cheese is melted.

SPOON Fiesta Salsa over tostaditas; top with additional topping suggestions.
Makes 8 servings.

For Fiesta Salsa:
COMBINE 1¾ cups (16-ounce jar) ORTEGA Thick & Chunky Salsa, 1 cup whole kernel corn and ½ cup (about 2 large) chopped green onions in medium bowl.

Ortega-Style Green Beans
EJOTES A LA ORTEGA

Mexican cookery offers a bounty of fresh vegetables. This is the Ortega-family way to eat green beans: with tomatoes, garlic, onions and green chiles.

- **1 tablespoon vegetable oil**
- **½ cup chopped onion**
- **2 cloves garlic, finely chopped**
- **1 pound fresh green beans, cut into 2-inch pieces, or 2 packages (9 ounces *each*) frozen green beans**
- **1¾ cups (14.5-ounce can) CONTADINA Dalla Casa Buitoni Recipe Ready Diced Tomatoes, undrained**
- **½ cup (4-ounce can) ORTEGA Diced Green Chiles**
- **½ teaspoon salt**

HEAT oil in large skillet over medium-high heat. Add onion and garlic; cook, stirring occasionally, for 1 to 2 minutes. Add beans, tomatoes and juice, chiles and salt. Bring to a boil. Reduce heat to low; cover. Cook, stirring occasionally, until beans are tender: 30 to 40 minutes for fresh beans, 10 to 12 minutes for frozen beans. Makes 6 servings.

Cream Cheese Flan
FLAN DE QUESO

This version of the traditional Mexican baked custard has an extra-creamy texture and rich flavor. It's ideal for entertaining, too. You can prepare it up to two days ahead.

- ¾ **cup granulated sugar**
- 1½ **cups (12 fluid-ounce can) CARNATION Evaporated Milk**
- 1¼ **cups (14-ounce can) CARNATION Sweetened Condensed Milk**
- 1 **package (8 ounces) cream cheese, softened, cut into chunks**
- 5 **eggs**

PLACE sugar in small, heavy-duty saucepan. Cook over medium-high heat, stirring constantly, for 3 to 4 minutes or until sugar is dissolved and golden. Quickly pour into eight 10-ounce custard cups;★ tip cups to coat bottoms and sides with sugar syrup.

PLACE evaporated milk, sweetened condensed milk and cream cheese in food processor or blender container; cover. Process until smooth. Add eggs; process until well mixed. Pour mixture into prepared cups. Place cups in two large baking pans; fill pans with hot water to 1-inch depth.

BAKE in preheated 350°F. oven for 30 to 40 minutes or until knife inserted in centers comes out clean. Remove to wire racks to cool for 30 minutes; chill for several hours or overnight. To serve, run small spatula around edges of cups; gently shake flans to loosen. Invert onto serving dishes to serve. Makes 8 servings.

★NOTE: To make one large flan, use one 2-quart casserole dish instead of custard cups. Coat with melted sugar syrup and pour milk mixture into dish as above. Place dish in large baking pan; fill pan halfway with hot water. Bake in preheated 350°F. oven for 60 to 70 minutes or until knife inserted in center comes out clean. Cool. Chill; invert as above onto a serving platter. Slice into wedges. Makes 8 servings.

Flan: The Classic Mexican Dessert

Mexico's dessert heritage came not from the oven, but from the stovetop. Its most famous dessert, the caramel-coated baked custard called flan, was originally cooked in a hot-water bath on top of the stove. Today it's usually baked in the oven. Although flan is a Spanish import, it is now nearly synonymous with Mexican cuisine.

The enticing dishes in this meal have been served in the Ortega family for generations. Once you sample the hearty enchiladas topped with pickled vegetables and the vermicelli, you'll want to serve them often in your home, too.

Ortega Family Favorites

Tortilla Chips with Ortega Salsa

Chicken Enchiladas with Pickled Vegetables

Ortega Family Vermicelli

Chocolate Cake

Milk

Chicken Enchiladas with Pickled Vegetables (front)
Ortega Family Vermicelli (back) (recipes pages 36 and 37)

Chicken Enchiladas with Pickled Vegetables
ENCHILADAS DE POLLO CON VERDURAS A LA VINAGRETA

The combination of tangy and spicy is a hallmark of Mexican cuisine. For these enchiladas, the tang comes from the pickled vegetables and the cheese; the spiciness from the salsa and the enchilada sauce.

Pickled Vegetables
- 1 cup (1 small) peeled chopped potato
- 1 cup (1 large) peeled chopped carrot
- 1 cup (1 small) chopped onion
- ½ cup ORTEGA Thick & Chunky Salsa, hot, medium or mild
- 2 tablespoons red wine vinegar

Enchiladas
- 2½ cups (about 3 large half breasts) cooked shredded chicken breast meat
- 1¼ cups (10-ounce can) ORTEGA Enchilada Sauce, *divided*
- ¼ cup vegetable oil
- 8 (6-inch) corn tortillas
- ¾ cup (3 ounces) shredded Monterey Jack cheese or queso fresco
- Fresh cilantro sprigs (optional)

For Pickled Vegetables:
PLACE potato, carrot and onion in medium saucepan; cover with water. Bring to a boil. Reduce heat to medium-low; cook, uncovered, for 10 to 12 minutes or until vegetables are crisp-tender. Drain. Combine vegetables, salsa and vinegar in medium bowl; mix well. Cover; chill for 1 hour.

For Enchiladas:
COMBINE chicken and ¼ *cup* enchilada sauce in medium bowl. Pour *remaining* enchilada sauce into small skillet; heat until warm.

HEAT oil in separate small skillet over medium-high heat for 2 to 3 minutes. Pass tortillas, using tongs, through oil to soften. Place on paper towels to soak. Pass tortillas through enchilada sauce in skillet.

PLACE ¼ cup chicken mixture down center of each tortilla; roll up. Place seam-side down on microwave-safe platter or baking dish. Top with *remaining* enchilada sauce; sprinkle with cheese. Heat in preheated 350°F. oven for 10 to 15 minutes or microwave on HIGH (100%) power for 4 to 5 minutes or until cheese is melted. Top with pickled vegetables. Garnish with cilantro. Makes 4 servings.

Ortega Family Vermicelli
FIDEO A LA ORTEGA

Fideo is the most popular pasta dish in Mexico. Each cook has his or her own special recipe; this fideo recipe is the Ortega family's version of this classic.

- 2 tablespoons vegetable oil
- 1 cup (1 small) chopped onion
- 3 cloves garlic, finely chopped
- 8 ounces fideo (coil vermicelli pasta), broken into pieces
- 1¾ cups (14.5-ounce can) CONTADINA Dalla Casa Buitoni Recipe Ready Diced Tomatoes, undrained
- 1¾ cups (14½-ounce can) chicken broth
- 1 cup (7-ounce can) ORTEGA Diced Green Chiles
- ½ teaspoon salt
- ⅛ teaspoon ground black pepper
- Crumbled cotija or feta cheese (optional)

HEAT oil in large skillet over medium-high heat. Add onion and garlic; cook, stirring occasionally, for 2 to 3 minutes or until onion is tender. Add pasta; cook, stirring constantly, for 1 to 2 minutes or until pasta starts to turn golden.

STIR in tomatoes and juice, broth, chiles, salt and pepper. Bring to a boil. Reduce heat to low; cook, stirring occasionally, for 5 to 7 minutes or until liquid is absorbed. Sprinkle with cheese just before serving. Makes 4 servings.

Chicken Broth Options

No chicken broth is more flavorful than one that's homemade. So here's a recipe to make your own:

Combine in a large stockpot: 6 cups cold water; 2½ pounds bone-in chicken pieces; 3 cut up stalks celery with leaves; 2 cut up carrots; 1 cut up large onion; 2 sprigs fresh parsley; 2 bay leaves; 1 teaspoon salt; and ¼ teaspoon ground black pepper. Bring to a boil. Reduce heat to low. Cover; cook for 2 hours. Remove chicken; set aside. Remove vegetables; discard. Strain the broth through a sieve (the meat from the bones can be used in other recipes). Store the broth in the refrigerator for up to 2 days or in the freezer for up to 1 month, or use it in a recipe such as the one above.

Homemade broth is nice to have on hand, but when you're short on time, you can opt for either canned broth or Maggi Bouillon Cubes dissolved in water.

Pasta, Mexican Style

Though pasta is not as widely prepared in Mexican cuisine as in Italian cooking, fideo (a very fine vermicelli) is considered standard fare.

This recipe is a sopa seca de fideo (a "dry soup" made with fideo). It is typically served as a pasta side dish. The most popular pasta dish is a soup called Sopa de Fideo (recipe page 67), which can be prepared in many ways. It is often a brothy soup that uses tomatoes and chiles in some form.

A difference between Italian and Mexican pasta: Fideo is traditionally cooked until slightly softer than the Italian al dente consistency.

The Ortega family proudly celebrates its culinary heritage

with this seafood menu. Complement the classic recipe, Fish Veracruz,

with either tortilla soup or Creamy Avocado

and Green Chile Soup.

Ortega Heritage Dinner

Tortilla, Green Chile and Lime Soup

~ *or* ~

Avocado and Green Chile Soup

Fish Veracruz

Couscous

Berry Pie

Sparkling Water

Fish Veracruz
Tortilla, Green Chile and Lime Soup
(recipes pages 40 and 41)

Tortilla, Green Chile and Lime Soup

SOPA DE TORTILLAS, CHILES VERDES Y LIMA

Mexico's famous flatbread, the tortilla, lends its name to the country's most famous soup. The fresh lime juice in this version is an influence from the Yucatán region of Mexico.

1 tablespoon vegetable oil
1 cup (1 small) quartered, sliced onion
2 cloves garlic, finely chopped
8 cups chicken broth
1¾ cups (14.5-ounce can) CONTADINA Dalla Casa Buitoni Recipe Ready Diced Tomatoes, drained
½ cup (4-ounce can) ORTEGA Diced Green Chiles
½ cup lime juice
½ teaspoon salt
2 cups (about 4 small half breasts) cooked shredded chicken breast meat
2 cups (about 2 ounces) tortilla chips, broken into pieces
Chopped avocado (optional)
Chopped fresh cilantro (optional)

HEAT oil in large saucepan over medium-high heat. Add onion and garlic; cook, stirring occasionally, for 3 to 4 minutes or until onion is tender. Add broth, tomatoes, chiles, lime juice and salt. Bring to a boil. Reduce heat to low; cook, uncovered, for 8 to 10 minutes. Add chicken; cook for 3 to 4 minutes.

LADLE soup into bowls. Top with tortilla chips, avocado and cilantro before serving. Makes 8 to 10 servings.

Avocado and Green Chile Soup

SOPA DE AGUACATE Y CHILES VERDES

The mellow flavors of this creamy, warming soup, sparked by a dollop of zesty salsa, make it a perfect first course to dinner.

3 large ripe avocados, peeled, seeded
½ onion, quartered
4 cups chicken broth
1 cup half-and-half or whole milk
½ cup (4-ounce can) ORTEGA Diced Green Chiles
1 teaspoon ground cumin
¾ teaspoon garlic salt
½ teaspoon ground white pepper
ORTEGA Thick & Chunky Salsa (optional)
Chopped fresh cilantro (optional)

PLACE avocado and onion in food processor or blender container; cover. Process until onion is coarsely chopped.

COMBINE broth and half-and-half in large saucepan. Bring to a boil over medium-high heat; reduce heat to low. Stir in avocado mixture, chiles, cumin, garlic salt and white pepper. Cook, stirring occasionally, for 2 to 3 minutes or until warm. Ladle into bowls. Top with salsa and cilantro before serving. Makes 8 servings.

Fish Veracruz

PESCADO A LA VERACRUZANA

The combination of piquant capers, olives and tongue-tingling chiles has brought this dish and its Gulf-side home of Veracruz worldwide recognition.

Fish
- 1½ **pounds red snapper or halibut fillets**
- ½ **cup lime juice**
- ½ **teaspoon salt**

Sauce
- 2 **tablespoons vegetable oil**
- 1 **cup (1 small) sliced onion**
- 1 **cup (1 small) green bell pepper strips**
- 3 **cloves garlic, finely chopped**
- ⅓ **cup dry white wine**
- 2½ **cups (24-ounce jar) ORTEGA Thick & Chunky Salsa, mild**
- ½ **cup CONTADINA Dalla Casa Buitoni Tomato Sauce**
- ¼ **cup ORTEGA Pickled Jalapeño Slices**
- ¼ **cup sliced ripe olives**
- 1 **tablespoon CROSSE & BLACKWELL Capers**
  Fresh cilantro sprigs (optional)
  Lime wedges (optional)

For Fish:
ARRANGE fish in 13 x 9-inch baking pan. Sprinkle with lime juice and salt; cover. Chill for at least 20 minutes.

For Sauce:
HEAT oil in large skillet over medium-high heat. Add onion, bell pepper and garlic; cook, stirring occasionally, for 1 to 2 minutes or until vegetables are crisp-tender. Add wine; cook for 1 minute.

STIR in salsa, tomato sauce, jalapeños, olives and capers. Bring to a boil. Place fish in sauce. Reduce heat to low. Cook, covered, for 8 to 10 minutes or until fish flakes when tested with fork. Serve with cilantro and lime. Makes 8 servings.

Cooking Fresh Fish

Sooner is better when it comes to cooking fresh fish. If that's not possible, wrap it loosely in clear plastic wrap and store it in the coldest part of the refrigerator for up to 2 days. Frozen fish can be kept in a freezer set at 0°F. or colder for up to 3 months.

When you do cook your fish, there are a couple of easy ways to tell when it is done. Properly cooked fish will look opaque rather than translucent, and will have milky-white juices. It will also flake easily when tested with a fork. If it resists flaking, or if the juices are clear and watery, it needs to cook a little longer.

The Spanish Influence

The landing of Spanish explorer Hernando Cortez in 1519 in the colonial port of Veracruz yielded one good consequence: From Mediterranean Spain came the olives and capers for Mexico's most famous seafood dish, snapper Veracruz.

A typical repast in Veracruz begins with sopa de camarón (shrimp soup) followed by Veracruz-style red snapper and picada—tortillas smothered with spicy red sauce and topped with chopped onion or beans and cheese.

The meal is finished with a steaming café con leche (coffee with milk).

Start the day with extra zest by

sharing this enticing brunch with friends and family.

You can serve as many as ten people with either

of these egg main dishes.

Mexican-Style Brunch

Ortega Ranch-Style Eggs
~ *or* ~
Shredded Beef with Eggs and Tortillas

Tropical Fruit

Coffee Cake

Mexican Milk Drink

Ortega Ranch-Style Eggs
Mexican Milk Drink
(recipes pages 44 and 45)

The Golden Egg

Huevos rancheros or "eggs, ranch-style" refers to the embellishment of cooked eggs with a chunky, rustic salsa. It's extremely popular in Mexico, as is the ubiquitous egg in its nearly countless forms.

Throughout Mexico, at any time of the day, people dine heartily on eggs. They might eat scrambled eggs in tomato sauce; scrambled eggs with black beans, chorizo, serrano peppers, tomatoes and onions, all rolled into a freshly made tortilla; omelets in red-chile sauce; baked eggs with oysters and shrimp; or scrambled eggs with shredded beef and a light chile sauce or salsa.

Ortega Ranch-Style Eggs

HUEVOS RANCHEROS A LA ORTEGA

Accompanied by warmed Ortega Refried Beans, this Mexican breakfast classic might just satisfy you until dinner. To make sure the tostada shells are as crisp as possible, serve them right after heating.

  2 tablespoons vegetable oil
  1 small onion, cut into thin wedges
  1 cup (1 small) sliced green or red bell pepper
  2 cloves garlic, finely chopped
1¾ cups (16-ounce jar) ORTEGA Garden Style Salsa, medium or mild
  ½ cup (4-ounce can) ORTEGA Diced Green Chiles
  ¼ teaspoon ground oregano
  1 package (10) ORTEGA Tostada Shells, warmed
10 fried or poached eggs*
  1 cup (4 ounces) shredded cheddar or Monterey Jack cheese
    Sliced green onions (optional)

HEAT oil in large skillet over medium-high heat. Add onion, bell pepper and garlic; cook, stirring occasionally, for 3 to 4 minutes or until vegetables are tender and onions are slightly golden.

ADD salsa, chiles and oregano. Bring to a boil. Remove from heat.

TOP each tostada shell with ⅓ cup sauce, 1 egg, cheese and green onions.
Makes 10 servings.

*NOTE: To fry eggs, melt 2 teaspoons butter or margarine in large skillet over medium heat. Break 5 eggs into skillet. When egg whites are set, add 1 to 2 teaspoons water. Cover; cook for 3 to 4 minutes or until yolks begin to thicken but are not hard. Remove eggs from skillet. Repeat with *remaining* eggs and additional butter.

  To poach eggs, add enough water to half-fill large, greased skillet. Bring to a boil. Reduce heat to simmer (bubbles should begin to break surface of water). Carefully break 1 egg into small dish or measuring cup. While holding lip of dish as close to water as possible, carefully slide egg into simmering water. Repeat with 4 more eggs, allowing each egg equal amount of space. Cook, uncovered, for about 5 minutes or until yolks are set. Remove eggs with slotted spoon. Repeat with *remaining* eggs.

Shredded Beef with Eggs and Tortillas

MACHACA CON HUEVOS Y TORTILLAS

Fill the tortillas with the beef-egg mixture, then top them with salsa and cheese, or eat the tortillas and beef separately, side by side.

- 1 tablespoon butter or margarine
- 6 eggs, lightly beaten
- 2 cups Shredded Beef Filling (recipe page 108)
- 10 (8-inch) soft taco-size flour tortillas, warmed
- 1¾ cups (1-pound can) ORTEGA Refried Beans, warmed (optional)
- 1 cup (4 ounces) shredded cheddar or Monterey Jack cheese
  ORTEGA Thick & Chunky Salsa, mild

HEAT butter in large skillet over medium-high heat. Add eggs; cook, stirring frequently, for 2 to 3 minutes or until eggs just begin to set.

STIR in Shredded Beef Filling. Cook, stirring occasionally, for 2 to 3 minutes or until eggs are cooked and beef is heated through. Serve with tortillas, beans, cheese and salsa. Makes 10 servings.

Mexican Milk Drink

ATOLE DE LECHE

Masa—dried-corn flour—gives body to atole, a hot beverage that is as creamy as a milkshake. This vanilla- and cinnamon-flavored version could be the base for many flavors of atole, such as chocolate, almond, peanut, strawberry, orange or tangerine.

- 3 cups water
- 1 cup masa harina flour (Mexican corn masa mix)
- 3¾ cups whole or low-fat milk
- 1½ cups (12 fluid-ounce can) CARNATION Evaporated Milk
- 1 cup granulated sugar
- 2 teaspoons vanilla extract
- 3 cinnamon sticks
  Cinnamon sticks (optional)

PLACE water and masa harina in blender container; cover. Blend until smooth. Pour through fine mesh sieve into medium saucepan. Bring to a boil. Reduce heat to low; cook, stirring frequently with wire whisk, for 6 to 8 minutes or until mixture is thickened.

STIR in whole milk, evaporated milk, sugar, vanilla and 3 cinnamon sticks. Bring to a boil. Reduce heat to low; cook, stirring frequently, for 5 to 8 minutes or until mixture is thickened. Remove cinnamon sticks. Serve warm with additional cinnamon sticks. Makes 10 servings.

Great Meals
With Great

Ortega Chicken Fajitas
(recipe page 50)

Friends

Everyone loves fiestas—especially those with generous helpings of hot foods and lively conversations. Sizzling fajitas, spicy Mexican meatballs and savory chicken mole are among the festive, easy-to-make recipes contained in the next menus. These are sure to be a hit at your next friendly gathering.

In this menu, guests can create their own fajitas by layering succulent chicken, colorful vegetables and an array of tantalizing toppings onto tortillas.

Festive Fajita Dinner

Ortega Family Green Chile Dip

Ortega Chicken Fajitas

Mexican Rice

Melon Wedges

Water with Fresh Lime Slices

Ortega Chicken Fajitas
Mexican Rice
(recipes pages 50 and 51)

Ortega Chicken Fajitas
FAJITAS DE POLLO A LA ORTEGA

Fajitas are a no-fail party food. They're easy to make and are perfect for guests who appreciate low-fat menu options.

  1 **tablespoon vegetable oil**
  1 **pound chicken breast meat, cut into thin strips**
  1 **cup (1 small) quartered, sliced onion**
  1 **cup (1 small) red and green bell pepper strips**
  1 **package (1.25 ounces) ORTEGA Fajita Seasoning Mix**
⅓ **cup water**
    Additional Ingredient Suggestions: warmed flour tortillas, chopped tomatoes, ORTEGA Green Chile Guacamole (recipe page 123), shredded cheese, ORTEGA Thick & Chunky Salsa and chopped fresh cilantro

HEAT oil in large skillet over medium-high heat. Add chicken; cook, stirring occasionally, for 4 to 5 minutes or until no longer pink on outside. Add onion and bell pepper; cook, stirring frequently, for 1 to 2 minutes or until chicken is no longer pink in center.

STIR in fajita seasoning mix and water. Bring to a boil. Reduce heat to low; cook for 2 to 3 minutes or until mixture is thickened.

SERVE with additional ingredient suggestions. Makes 8 servings.

Creating Your Own Fajitas

In the old days, fajitas were made only with beef skirt or flank steak, but they easily lend themselves to variety. Instead of the chicken used in the above recipe, try marinated beef, pork loin, shrimp or even a firm white fish like shark or swordfish cut into 2-inch chunks. Vary the vegetables, too. Besides red, green and yellow bell pepper strips and onion, opt for zucchini, yellow squash or jicama strips.

Fajitas are best served fresh while the tortillas are still warm. Simply place a portion of the meat and vegetable mixture on the tortilla. Garnish with chopped tomatoes, guacamole, sour cream, shredded cheese, salsa and chopped fresh cilantro, then roll it up.

The Original Fajita

Fajitas are a quick-seared Tex-Mex interpretation of Mexican carne asada—very thin strips of beef cooked over charcoal, then wrapped in fresh tortillas.

The word "fajitas" refers to the cut of beef—usually called skirt steak—from which the strips are sliced. The cut looks like a fajo, or belt. Skirt steak is the cut of beef just above the tenderloin.

Fajitas were popularized in the 1970s by Texans, and soon fajitas were sizzling on grills and in frying pans across the country.

Mexican Rice

ARROZ MEXICANO

This classic dish, found in every region of Mexico, is referred to as a "dry soup" because the rice is cooked in a savory soup-like liquid. As it cooks, the rice soaks up the liquid—and, correspondingly, the flavor and color of the tomatoes and chiles.

- 2 tablespoons (¼ stick) butter or margarine
- 1 cup long-grain white rice★
- ½ cup chopped onion
- 2 cloves garlic, finely chopped
- 1¾ cups (16-ounce jar) ORTEGA Thick & Chunky Salsa, hot, medium or mild
- 1¼ cups water★
- ¾ cup peeled shredded carrot
- ½ cup frozen peas, thawed (optional)

MELT butter in large saucepan over medium heat. Add rice, onion and garlic; cook, stirring occasionally, for 3 to 4 minutes or until rice is golden. Stir in salsa, water, carrot and peas. Bring to a boil. Reduce heat to low; cook, covered, for 25 to 30 minutes or until liquid is absorbed and rice is tender. Makes 8 servings.

★NOTE: For a quick-cook Mexican Rice, use 4 cups instant rice instead of 1 cup long-grain white rice, and 2½ cups water instead of 1¼ cups water. After salsa mixture comes to a boil, cook for length of time recommended on instant rice package.

Ortega Family Green Chile Dip

This cool, creamy, easy-to-make dip is an Ortega-family favorite. As it simply sits and chills in the refrigerator, the chiles infuse the sour cream with their piquant flavor.

- 2 cups sour cream
- 1 cup (7-ounce can) ORTEGA Diced Green Chiles
- ½ teaspoon garlic salt
- Tortilla chips

COMBINE sour cream, chiles and garlic salt in medium bowl; cover. Chill for 2 to 4 hours or overnight until flavors are blended. Serve with chips. Makes 2¾ cups.

Delight friends and family with home cooking Mexican style.

Take your pick of either the flavorful meatballs in a zesty sauce

or the jalapeño-seasoned meatloaf. Finish with a rich,

velvety chocolate pudding.

Spicy Dinner

Meatballs in Chile Sauce
~ *or* ~
Meatloaf Mexicana

Rice

Steamed Green Beans

Cinnamon Chocolate Pudding

Coffee or Tea

Meatballs in Chile Sauce
(recipe page 54)

Meatballs in Chile Sauce
ALBÓNDIGAS EN SALSA PICANTE

Chipotle chiles are smoked, dried jalapeño peppers that are available canned in adobo (mild red chile) sauce, pickled or dried. Use additional chiles for more heat, but remember, a little chipotle goes a long way!

Meatballs
- 1½ **pounds ground beef**
- 1 **cup (1 small) chopped onion**
- ¼ **cup CONTADINA Dalla Casa Buitoni Seasoned Bread Crumbs**
- 2 **eggs, lightly beaten**
- 3 **tablespoons chopped fresh parsley**
- 1 **tablespoon sauce from canned chipotle chiles in adobo sauce or ORTEGA Thick & Chunky Salsa**
- ½ **teaspoon salt**

Sauce
- 2½ **cups (24-ounce jar) ORTEGA Thick & Chunky Salsa**
- 1 **cup water**
- ⅔ **cup (6-ounce can) CONTADINA Dalla Casa Buitoni Tomato Paste**
- 2 **cloves garlic, finely chopped**
- 1 to 2 **canned chipotle chiles in adobo sauce, finely chopped (optional)**
- 1 **MAGGI Chicken Bouillon Cube**
- **Cooked rice (optional)**
- **Green onion curl (optional)**

For Meatballs:
COMBINE beef, onion, bread crumbs, eggs, parsley, chile sauce and salt in large bowl; mix well. Form mixture into 18 meatballs.

For Sauce:
COMBINE salsa, water, tomato paste, garlic, chiles and bouillon in large saucepan. Bring to a boil. Reduce heat to medium-low. Place meatballs in sauce; cook, stirring occasionally, for 20 to 25 minutes or until meatballs are no longer pink in center. Serve with rice. Garnish with green onion curl. Makes 6 servings.

Meatball Soup

Without the chipotle sauce, these flavorful meatballs, which also can be made with ground pork, or half beef and half pork, are often incorporated into a light and satisfying soup that is a favorite in Mexico for a mid-morning pick-me-up or brunch.

For Sopa de Albóndigas (meatball soup), chicken or beef broth is embellished with cumin, oregano, chopped tomatoes, zucchini, carrots, onions, chiles and cilantro. Add the meatballs and gently simmer until they are cooked through.

 ### Shaping Meatballs Easily

Whether you're making Mexican, Italian or Swedish meatballs, the method for shaping them is the same.

To make sure your meatballs are similar in size so they cook evenly, try the following trick: For 1-inch meatballs, shape the seasoned meat mixture into a square 1 inch thick, then cut the square into 1-inch pieces. Correspondingly, for 1½-inch meatballs, shape the meat mixture into a 1½-inch-thick square and cut into 1½-inch cubes. Roll each cube into a ball.

Meatloaf Mexicana

This interpretation of an American classic both breaks and embraces tradition. Embellished with cheese, Ortega Thick & Chunky Salsa and fiery jalapeños, it elevates everyday meatloaf from basic to bold.

- 1 pound ground pork
- ¾ pound ground beef
- 1¼ cups (5 ounces) shredded Monterey Jack cheese or queso fresco, *divided*
- 1 cup plain dried bread crumbs
- 2 eggs, lightly beaten
- 1 cup ORTEGA Thick & Chunky Salsa, mild, *divided*
- 1 tablespoon chopped fresh parsley
- 2 teaspoons ORTEGA Diced Jalapeños
- 1 teaspoon salt

COMBINE pork, beef, *1 cup* cheese, bread crumbs, eggs, *½ cup* salsa, parsley, jalapeños and salt in large bowl. Place meat mixture into lightly greased 9 x 5-inch loaf pan.

BAKE in preheated 350°F. oven for 55 to 60 minutes or until no longer pink in center. Remove from oven; drain. Cool on wire rack for 10 minutes; remove from pan. Top with *remaining* salsa and cheese before serving. Makes 6 servings.

Cinnamon Chocolate Pudding
PUDÍN DE CHOCOLATE Y CANELA

Nothing cools the palate more sweetly after a spicy meal than a smooth, creamy pudding— and there's no more fitting flavor to follow Mexican food than chocolate.

- ½ cup granulated sugar
- 2 tablespoons cornstarch
- 1 teaspoon ground cinnamon
- 2 cans (12 fluid-ounces *each*) CARNATION Evaporated Milk
- 1¼ cups (6 ounces) NESTLÉ TOLL HOUSE Semi-Sweet Chocolate Morsels
- 2 egg yolks, lightly beaten
- ½ cup flaked coconut, toasted

COMBINE sugar, cornstarch and cinnamon in medium saucepan; gradually stir in evaporated milk. Stir in morsels and egg yolks. Bring to a boil over medium heat, stirring constantly, until mixture is thickened.

POUR chocolate mixture into dessert cups. Chill for at least 1 hour; sprinkle with coconut. Makes 8 servings.

With this hearty dinner, your guests can eat their fill in the tradition of the vaqueros (Mexican cowboys) of years ago. Chimichangas brimming with beef and a side of Cowboy Beans make a mouthwatering meal you'll want to serve often.

Ranch-Style Supper

Beef Chimichangas

Cowboy Beans

Ortega Apple and Green Chile Salad

Brownies

Lemonade or Iced Tea

Beef Chimichangas
Cowboy Beans
Ortega Apple and Green Chile Salad
(recipes pages 58 and 59)

Beef Chimichangas
CHIMICHANGAS DE CARNE

Chimichangas are simply burritos fried until crisp and golden. They can be filled with beef, chicken or refried beans.

> 1 **pound ground beef**
> 1 **package (8) ORTEGA Burrito Dinner Kit (flour tortillas, burrito seasoning mix), tortillas warmed**
> 1¾ **cups water**
> 1 **cup (4 ounces) shredded cheddar cheese**
> **Vegetable oil**
> **ORTEGA Thick & Chunky Salsa, hot, medium or mild**
> **ORTEGA Green Chile Guacamole (recipe page 123) (optional)**

COOK ground beef in medium skillet over medium-high heat, stirring often, for 4 to 5 minutes or until no longer pink; drain. Stir in burrito seasoning mix and water. Bring to a boil. Reduce heat to low; cook, stirring constantly, for 5 to 6 minutes or until beef mixture is thickened.

PLACE beef mixture evenly on each tortilla; sprinkle with cheese. Fold into burritos (see tip page 86); secure ends with wooden picks. Add oil to 1-inch depth in medium skillet; heat over high heat for 3 to 4 minutes. Place 1 or 2 burritos in oil; fry, turning frequently with tongs, for 1 to 2 minutes or until golden brown. Place on paper towels to soak. Remove wooden picks. Serve with salsa and guacamole. Makes 8 servings.

Ortega Apple and Green Chile Salad
ENSALADA DE MANZANAS Y CHILES VERDES

A creative cook in the Ortega family combined spicy chiles with cool, crisp celery and apples in a creamy dressing. The resulting salad is a symphony of tastes and textures.

> 2 **cups (2 medium) chopped red and green apples**
> 1 **cup (2 stalks) sliced celery**
> ½ **cup chopped walnuts, toasted**
> ½ **cup (4-ounce can) ORTEGA Diced Green Chiles**
> ⅓ **cup prepared ranch-style salad dressing**
> ¼ **cup mayonnaise**
> **Lettuce leaves (optional)**

COMBINE apples, celery, nuts, chiles, salad dressing and mayonnaise in medium bowl; cover. Chill for 1 hour. Serve on bed of lettuce. Makes 8 servings.

Cowboy Beans
Frijoles Charros

In Mexico, this savory dish is served as an accompaniment to a variety of grilled meats and chicken.

      4 quarts water
   2½ cups (1 pound) dry pinto beans, rinsed, sorted, soaked and drained
      1 small onion, quartered
      1 tablespoon salt
      1 pound ground beef
    10 ounces longaniza-style chorizo, casing removed, crumbled
      1 cup (1 small) chopped onion
      1 cup (1 large) chopped green bell pepper
      3 cloves garlic, finely chopped
   1¾ cups (14.5-ounce can) CONTADINA Dalla Casa Buitoni Recipe
          Ready Diced Tomatoes, undrained
    ⅔ cup (6-ounce can) CONTADINA Dalla Casa Buitoni Tomato Paste
      1 package (1.25 ounces) ORTEGA Fajita Seasoning Mix

PLACE water, beans and quartered onion in large stockpot. Bring to a boil. Reduce heat to low; cook, partially covered, for 1½ hours or until beans are tender. Add salt; cook for additional 30 minutes.

COMBINE beef, chorizo, chopped onion, bell pepper and garlic in large skillet. Cook over medium-high heat, stirring occasionally, for 5 to 6 minutes or until vegetables are tender and beef is no longer pink; drain.

ADD beef mixture, tomatoes and juice, tomato paste and fajita seasoning mix to beans. Mix well; cover. Cook over medium heat, stirring occasionally, for 30 minutes.
Makes about 8 servings.

Preparing Dried Beans

To make them tender, dried beans need to be soaked before cooking. If you have the time, simply place them in a bowl, cover with cold water and place them in the refrigerator to soak overnight.

Or, you can quick-soak the beans: Rinse beans. Combine 1 pound beans and 8 cups cold water in large stockpot. Bring to a boil. Reduce heat to low; cook for 2 minutes. Remove from heat; cover. Let stand for 1 hour; proceed with recipe or cook as follows:

Drain soaked beans; rinse. Combine beans and 8 cups fresh water in stockpot. Bring to a boil; reduce heat to low. Cover; cook for 1 to 1¾ hours. Beans are done when they are soft.

Full of Beans

Along with rice, chiles and corn, beans are a fundamental presence in Mexican cookery. Most frequently found on the Mexican table are chickpeas (garbanzo beans) and red kidney, pinto and black beans. In the North, beans take on many forms: frijoles charros (cowboy beans), boiled over an open fire with peppers, herbs and sometimes bits of meat; frijoles borrachos (drunken beans), beans cooked with beer; and frijoles maneados; beans embellished with cheese and ancho chiles.

Whether you're celebrating a special wedding anniversary

or simply getting the neighbors together for a meal, this splendidly

seasoned menu will fit any occasion. Your guests will love the contrast of

the full-flavored chicken mole and delicate spoon bread.

Special Dinner Celebration

Chicken Mole

Corn with Tomatoes and Green Chiles

Rice with Parsley

Spoon Bread with Green Chiles

Mexican Almond Cookies

Sparkling Fruit Punch

Chicken Mole
Corn with Tomatoes and Green Chiles
Spoon Bread with Green Chiles
(recipes pages 62 and 63)

Chicken Mole

MOLE CON POLLO

Often considered the national dish of Mexico, mole is a rich, deep reddish brown sauce made from a blend of spices, chiles, nuts, seeds and a small amount of chocolate. Mole is most often served with chicken.

    2 tablespoons vegetable oil
    4 pounds chicken parts
    1 cup (1 small) chopped onion
    1 clove garlic, finely chopped
  2½ cups (24-ounce jar) ORTEGA Thick & Chunky Salsa, mild
    1 cup chicken broth
    3 tablespoons chili powder
    2 to 3 tablespoons creamy peanut butter
    2 tablespoons NESTLÉ TOLL HOUSE Baking Cocoa
    8 cups cooked long-grain white rice (optional)
      Chopped fresh parsley (optional)

HEAT oil in large skillet over medium-high heat. Add chicken; cook, turning frequently, for 4 to 6 minutes or until browned on all sides. Remove from skillet. Add onion and garlic; cook, stirring constantly, for 2 to 3 minutes or until onion is tender.

STIR in salsa, broth, chili powder, peanut butter and cocoa. Bring to a boil. Reduce heat to medium-low. Place chicken in sauce; cook, uncovered, for 20 to 25 minutes or until chicken is no longer pink near bone.

COMBINE rice and parsley in medium bowl; serve with Chicken Mole. Makes 8 servings.

Buying and Storing Chicken

Choosing the best part of the chicken to make chicken mole is easy—it's the cut you like best! Chickens are sold whole (to cut yourself), cut up or by the piece (all breasts or all thighs, for instance). You can also buy skinless chicken breasts, or chicken parts with the skin.

Chicken is highly perishable and requires a little vigilance in purchasing and storing. Be sure to check the "sell by" date on the label. That's the last day it should be sold. (If it's properly refrigerated, chicken will retain its freshness for a couple of days after that date.) Store fresh chicken in the coldest part of your refrigerator, and plan to use it within 1 to 2 days. Chicken that's packaged in a styrofoam tray can be refrigerated in its original wrapping.

More on Mole

The legend of the origin of mole is almost as rich as the distinctive sauce itself.

As the story goes, one Lenten Sunday in the 18th century, the bishop of Puebla invited the Spanish viceroy to dine at the convent of Santa Rosa, renowned for its fine cuisine. The cook, Sor Andrea de la Asunción, was asked to make a meal like no other. She set about combining anise, clove, cinnamon, black pepper and several varieties of chiles: ancho, mulato, pasilla and chipotle. She added fried garlic, piquant green tomatillos, tortillas, sesame seeds, ground almonds, peanuts and, as a final touch, a bit of bitter chocolate. As the thick sauce bubbled on the stove, the exotic flavors blended until they were melded to perfection. Sor Andrea then ladled her creation over corn-fed, chestnut-stuffed turkey.

Spoon Bread with Green Chiles

Spoon bread can't be sliced and buttered. This pudding-like casserole made with cornmeal is so soft and creamy, it has to be served and eaten with a spoon.

1½ **cups (12 fluid-ounce can) CARNATION Evaporated Milk**
¾ **cup water**
½ **cup ALBERS Yellow Corn Meal**
½ **teaspoon salt**
½ **cup (4-ounce can) ORTEGA Diced Green Chiles**
1 **tablespoon granulated sugar**
1 **tablespoon chopped fresh cilantro**
2 **eggs**
½ **cup (2 ounces) shredded cheddar cheese**
 ORTEGA Garden Style Salsa, mild

COMBINE evaporated milk, water, cornmeal and salt in large saucepan. Cook, stirring constantly, over medium-low heat until mixture is thickened. Remove mixture from heat.

STIR in chiles, sugar and cilantro. Add eggs, one at a time, stirring well after each addition. Pour into greased 1-quart ovenproof dish.

BAKE, uncovered, in preheated 350°F. oven for 20 to 25 minutes or until knife inserted near center comes out clean. Sprinkle with cheese; bake for additional 2 to 3 minutes or until cheese is melted. Serve with salsa. Makes 6 servings.

Corn with Tomatoes and Green Chiles

MAÍZ CON TOMATES Y CHILES VERDES

This brightly colored dish is a fresh way to serve corn—a Mexican staple. Substitute quartered cherry tomatoes for the chopped tomato if you like.

1 **tablespoon vegetable oil**
2 **cups whole kernel corn**
1 **cup (1 small) chopped onion**
1 **clove garlic, finely chopped**
1 **cup (1 medium) chopped tomato**
½ **cup (4-ounce can) ORTEGA Diced Green Chiles**
½ **teaspoon salt**

HEAT oil in large skillet over medium-high heat. Add corn, onion and garlic; cook, stirring occasionally, for 3 to 4 minutes or until onion is tender. Add tomato, chiles and salt; cook, stirring occasionally, for 1 to 2 minutes or until mixture is heated through. Makes 6 servings.

When you're having a large group over

for dinner, feed everyone easily with this satisfying soup menu.

Make two or three soups, then let guests enjoy their choice

of steaming soup with crisp relishes and

cheesy corn bread.

Soup Supper

Assorted Relishes with Dip

Chicken and Hominy Soup
~ *or* ~
Ortega Chile Verde
~ *or* ~
Vermicelli Soup

Fiesta Corn Bread

Fruit Tarts

Iced Tea

Chicken and Hominy Soup
Fiesta Corn Bread
(recipes page 66)

Chicken and Hominy Soup

POSOLE

This soup may be topped with cabbage, radishes, onion, oregano and lime.

      4 quarts water
  2½ to 3 pounds chicken parts
      2 pounds pork hocks
      1 onion, quartered
    2¾ cups (*two* 15-ounce cans) white hominy, drained
      1 cup (1 small) sliced onion
    1¾ cups (16-ounce jar) ORTEGA Thick & Chunky Salsa, *divided*
      1 teaspoon salt
      1 teaspoon dried oregano, crushed
      1 teaspoon ground cumin
         Shredded cabbage (optional)
         Tortilla strips (optional)

PLACE water, chicken, pork hocks and quartered onion in large stockpot; cover. Bring to a boil. Reduce heat to low; cook, partially covered, for 1½ hours or until meat begins to come off bones. Remove chicken and pork hocks from broth. Remove any meat from bones. Discard skin, bones and fat; chop meat. Chill broth for 1 hour or until fat is solidified. Strain broth into large saucepan through fine-mesh strainer.

ADD meat, hominy, sliced onion, ½ cup salsa, salt, oregano and cumin to broth; stir. Bring to a boil. Reduce heat to low; cook, uncovered, for 25 to 30 minutes or until flavors are blended.

SERVE in soup bowls topped with cabbage, *remaining* salsa and tortilla strips.
Makes 10 to 12 servings.

Fiesta Corn Bread

PAN DE MAÍZ

Diced green chiles and cheddar cheese spice up this Southwestern favorite.

    2¼ cups all-purpose flour
    1¾ cups ALBERS White or Yellow Corn Meal
    1½ cups (6 ounces) shredded cheddar cheese
      1 cup (7-ounce can) ORTEGA Diced Green Chiles
      ½ cup granulated sugar
      2 tablespoons baking powder
    1½ teaspoons salt
      2 cups milk
      ⅔ cup vegetable oil
      2 eggs, lightly beaten

COMBINE flour, cornmeal, cheese, chiles, sugar, baking powder and salt in large bowl. Add milk, oil and eggs; stir just until moistened. Spread into greased 13 x 9-inch baking pan.

BAKE in preheated 375°F. oven for 30 to 35 minutes or until wooden pick inserted in center comes out clean. Cool in pan for 10 minutes; cut into squares. Cut squares diagonally in half. Makes 24 servings.

The Making of Posole

Traditionally, this hearty pork and hominy stew was made with a pig's head. Pork hocks are decidedly easier!

Each region has its own version of posole. It comes, in fact, in the colors of the Mexican flag—red, white and green, depending on the kinds of chiles that are used to season it.

In certain parts of Mexico, one day a week is designated as "posole day." Shops close early, work comes to a stop and people retire to posole "restaurants"— which are temporary arrangements of tables and chairs—so everyone may partake of the rich stew served steaming in earthenware bowls.

Ortega Chile Verde

"Chile con carne" has been shortened to "chile," ("chili" north of the border), but it means the same thing: chiles with meat. Chile made with beef and red chiles may be most familiar, but this chile made with pork and green chiles is chile made the Ortega family way.

- 3 tablespoons vegetable oil
- 1 cup (1 small) chopped onion
- 3 cloves garlic, finely chopped
- 3 pounds pork tenderloin or boneless pork chops, cut into ½-inch pieces
- ¼ cup all-purpose flour
- 3½ cups (*two 14.5-ounce cans*) CONTADINA Dalla Casa Buitoni Recipe Ready Diced Tomatoes, undrained
- 2 cups (*two 7-ounce cans*) ORTEGA Diced Green Chiles
- ¾ cup chicken broth
- ½ teaspoon salt

HEAT oil in large saucepan over medium-high heat. Add onion and garlic; cook, stirring occasionally, for 2 to 3 minutes or until onions are tender. Add pork and flour; cook, stirring frequently, for 3 to 5 minutes or until pork is no longer pink on outside.

ADD tomatoes and juice, chiles, broth and salt. Bring to a boil. Reduce heat to medium-low; cover partially. Cook, stirring occasionally, for 15 to 20 minutes or until pork is no longer pink in center and sauce is thickened. Makes 6 to 8 servings.

Vermicelli Soup

SOPA DE FIDEO

Fideo (fine vermicelli) is used in both pasta dishes and soups. Garnish this main-dish soup with chopped fresh cilantro and shredded Monterey Jack cheese.

- 1 tablespoon vegetable oil
- 8 ounces fideo (coil vermicelli pasta), broken into pieces
- 5¼ cups (*three 14½-ounce cans*) chicken broth
- 2 cups water
- 1¾ cups (16-ounce jar) ORTEGA Thick & Chunky Salsa, mild
- 2 cups (about 4 medium half breasts) cooked, chopped chicken breast meat

HEAT oil in large saucepan over medium-high heat. Add pasta; cook, stirring constantly, for 3 to 4 minutes or until mixture begins to brown.

STIR in broth, water and salsa; cover. Bring to a boil. Reduce heat to medium; cook for 10 to 15 minutes or until pasta is tender. Add chicken; cook for 2 to 3 minutes or until heated through. Makes 10 servings.

One-Dish

Shrimp Enchiladas (front) (recipe page 70)
Enchilada Stacks (back right) (recipe page 71)
Enchilada Casserole (back left) (recipe page 71)

Dinners

Mexican cookery has a tradition of serving hearty, flavorful one-dish dinners. These menus are perfect family fare with a crisp and colorful taco salad, a tamale pie and three quick-to-fix types of enchiladas. Try one of these recipes when you want something satisfying but are short on time.

Enchilada Dinner

Shrimp Enchiladas

~ *or* ~

Enchilada Casserole

~ *or* ~

Enchilada Stacks

Fresh Fruit Salad

Shrimp Enchiladas

ENCHILADAS DE CAMARÓN

Stuffed with tender bay shrimp, these enchiladas are lighter and more delicately flavored than their heartier, meat-filled cousins.

> 1 **tablespoon vegetable oil**
> 1 **cup (1 small) chopped onion**
> 1 **cup (1 large) chopped green bell pepper**
> 1 **clove garlic, finely chopped**
> 1¼ **cups (10-ounce can) ORTEGA Enchilada Sauce with Green Chiles & Onion,** *divided*
> ½ **pound cooked bay shrimp**
> ¼ **cup vegetable oil**
> 8 **(6-inch) corn tortillas**
> 1½ **cups (6 ounces) shredded Monterey Jack cheese,** *divided*
> **Sliced red chile pepper (optional)**

HEAT 1 tablespoon oil in medium skillet over medium-high heat. Add onion, bell pepper and garlic; cook, stirring occasionally, for 3 to 4 minutes or until vegetables are tender. Add ¼ *cup* enchilada sauce and shrimp. Cook for 2 minutes or until heated through. Pour *remaining* enchilada sauce into small skillet; heat until warm.

HEAT ¼ cup oil in separate small skillet over medium-high heat for 2 to 3 minutes. Pass tortillas, using tongs, through oil to soften. Place on paper towels to soak. Pass tortillas through enchilada sauce in skillet.

SPOON ¼ cup shrimp mixture down center of each tortilla; sprinkle with *1 tablespoon* cheese. Roll up. Place on microwave-safe platter or baking dish. Top with *remaining* enchilada sauce. Sprinkle with *remaining* cheese. Heat in preheated 350°F. oven for 5 to 8 minutes or microwave on HIGH (100%) power for 2 to 3 minutes or just until cheese is melted. Top with chile-pepper slices. Makes 4 servings.

Enchilada Casserole

This layered casserole provides a no-fuss way to capture all the tastes and textures of traditional enchiladas without dipping and rolling.

- 1 pound ground beef
- 1 cup (1 small) chopped onion
- 2 cloves garlic, finely chopped
- 2 cans (10 ounces *each*) ORTEGA Enchilada Sauce with Green Chiles & Onion
- ½ cup (2¼-ounce can) sliced ripe olives, drained, *divided*
- 10 (6-inch) corn tortillas, sliced in half, *divided*
- 2 cups (8 ounces) shredded cheddar cheese, *divided*
  Sliced green onions (optional)

COMBINE beef, onion and garlic in large skillet. Cook over medium-high heat, stirring occasionally, for 4 to 5 minutes or until meat is no longer pink; drain.

STIR in enchilada sauce and *¼ cup* olives. Bring to a boil. Reduce heat to low; cover. Cook, stirring frequently, for 5 to 8 minutes.

LAYER *half* of tortillas on bottom of greased 12 x 7-inch baking dish. Cover with *half* of meat sauce; sprinkle with *1 cup* cheese. Repeat layers. Bake, covered, in preheated 375°F. oven for 20 minutes. Remove cover; bake for additional 5 minutes or until bubbly and cheese is melted. Sprinkle with *remaining* olives and green onions. Makes 8 servings.

Enchilada Stacks

This simple recipe layers ingredients for great enchilada flavor. The stacks are cut into wedges and may be garnished with avocado slices.

- 12 (6-inch) corn tortillas
- 1¾ cups (1-pound can) ORTEGA Refried Beans with Green Chiles & Lime
- 1¼ cups (10-ounce can) ORTEGA Enchilada Sauce
- 1½ cups (3 ounces *each*) shredded cheddar and Monterey Jack cheese
- ½ cup (about 2 large) chopped green onions

HEAT tortillas, one at a time, in small skillet over medium-high heat for 30 seconds on each side or until soft. Place two warmed tortillas, side by side, on bottom of lightly greased 13 x 9-inch baking dish. Spread about 2 tablespoons beans over each tortilla. Top each with 1 tablespoon enchilada sauce, 2 tablespoons cheese and 2 teaspoons green onions. Repeat each layer until all tortillas are used, completing two stacks of six.

POUR *remaining* enchilada sauce over stacks. Bake, uncovered, in preheated 350°F. oven for 15 to 20 minutes or until heated through. Cut into wedges to serve. Makes 6 to 8 servings.

Enchiladas

In Spanish, to "enchilar" something is to get chiles all over it. Hence, the name for the much-beloved enchilada. Traditional preparation of enchiladas calls for corn tortillas to be quick-fried, then dipped in a chile sauce (a plain red-chile sauce, mole or tomatillo-chile sauce), filled and rolled.

Mexico is home to a variety of enchiladas—from hearty beef or bean-filled versions to the lighter street-food types that are stuffed with fried potato, carrot and cheese.

As with most Mexican dishes, there are distinct regional variations of enchiladas. There are also related dishes that are not technically enchiladas because they're not dipped in chile sauce, but they use the same technique of frying, dipping in sauce and rolling.

Among those are the Oaxacan enfrijoladas, which are dipped in a bean sauce; tomato-sauced entomatadas; and the stacked pan de cazón.

Salad Lunch

Mexican Taco Salad

Ortega Green Chile Guacamole
(recipe page 123)

Mexican Taco Salad

Even finicky kids will eat salad when taco ingredients are part of the equation.

    1 pound ground beef or turkey
    1 cup (1 small) chopped onion
    1 package (1.25 ounces) ORTEGA Taco Seasoning Mix
    1 cup ORTEGA Thick & Chunky Salsa, mild
    ¾ cup water
 1¾ cups (15-ounce can) kidney or pinto beans, rinsed, drained
    ½ cup (4-ounce can) ORTEGA Diced Green Chiles
    3 cups (3 ounces) tortilla chips
    6 cups torn lettuce
    1 cup (4 ounces) shredded cheddar cheese
      Tomato wedges (optional)
      Sour cream (optional)
      Sliced green onions (optional)

COMBINE beef and onion in large skillet. Cook over medium-high heat, stirring occasionally, for 4 to 5 minutes or until beef is no longer pink; drain.

ADD taco seasoning mix, salsa and water; mix well. Bring to a boil. Reduce heat to low; cook for 2 to 3 minutes. Stir in beans and chiles.

LAYER ingredients as follows on six plates: ½ cup chips, 1 cup lettuce, ¾ cup meat mixture, about 2 tablespoons cheese, tomato wedges, sour cream and green onions. Makes 6 servings.

Casserole Supper

Tamale Pie

Sliced Tomatoes

Tamale Pie
PASTEL DE TAMAL

For variety, substitute ground turkey for the ground beef in this family favorite.

- 1½ pounds ground beef
- 1 cup (1 small) chopped onion
- 2 cloves garlic, finely chopped
- 2 cans (10 ounces *each*) ORTEGA Enchilada Sauce with Onions
- 1 cup whole kernel corn
- ½ cup (2¼-ounce can) sliced ripe olives, drained
- 2 teaspoons salt, *divided*
- 2¼ cups ALBERS Yellow or White Corn Meal
- 2 cups water
- 1½ cups (12 fluid-ounce can) CARNATION Evaporated Milk
- ½ cup (4-ounce can) ORTEGA Diced Green Chiles
- ½ cup (2 ounces) shredded cheddar cheese
- ORTEGA Pickled Jalapeño Slices (optional)

COMBINE beef, onion and garlic in large skillet. Cook over medium-high heat, stirring occasionally, for 4 to 5 minutes or until beef is no longer pink; drain. Stir in enchilada sauce, corn, olives and *1 teaspoon* salt. Set aside.

COMBINE cornmeal, water, evaporated milk and *remaining* salt in medium saucepan. Cook over medium-high heat, stirring frequently, for 5 to 7 minutes or until thick. Stir in chiles. Reserve *2 cups* cornmeal mixture; cover with plastic wrap. Spread *remaining* cornmeal mixture on bottom and up sides of greased 12 x 7-inch baking dish. Bake in preheated 425°F. oven for 10 minutes. Cool on wire rack.

SPOON meat mixture into cornmeal crust. Spread reserved cornmeal mixture over meat filling. Bake in preheated 425°F. oven for 15 to 20 minutes; sprinkle with cheese. Bake for additional 5 to 10 minutes or until cheese is melted. Garnish with jalapeños. Makes 6 servings.

Skillet Chicken Dinner

Chicken in Stewed Tomato Sauce

Rice

Chicken in Stewed Tomato Sauce
POLLO ENJITOMATADO

Serve this easy main dish with arroz blanco (white rice) to soak up the delicious sauce. Substitute boneless chicken breasts for the thighs and legs in this recipe if you prefer.

> 2 tablespoons vegetable oil★
> 2 pounds (about 6) chicken thighs and legs
> 1 cup (1 small) quartered, sliced onion
> 1 cup (1 small) green bell pepper strips
> 2 cloves garlic, finely chopped
> 2¼ cups (24-ounce jar) ORTEGA Thick & Chunky Salsa, mild
> ½ cup chicken broth

HEAT oil in large skillet over medium-high heat. Add chicken; cook, turning frequently, for 5 to 6 minutes or until browned on all sides. Remove from skillet.

ADD onion, bell pepper and garlic to skillet; cook, stirring frequently, for 2 to 3 minutes or until vegetables are tender. Add salsa, broth and chicken. Bring to a boil. Reduce heat to low; cook, partially covered, for 25 to 30 minutes or until chicken is no longer pink near bone. Makes 6 servings.

★NOTE: If you're watching fat, you can make a little oil go a long way. When cooking foods in oil, it's important to coat the entire bottom of the skillet with oil to avoid sticking, but you can use a pastry brush to spread the oil, rather than adding more. To use even less oil, try using a nonstick skillet instead of a regular pan. You may still need some oil, but not as much as a regular skillet. For vegetables, you may be able to skip the fat entirely by cooking them in a small amount of broth or water.

Chimichanga Supper

Garden-Style Chicken Chimichangas

Ortega Refried Beans

Garden-Style Chicken Chimichangas

Light and fresh tasting, these crisp-fried, flour-tortilla pockets are packed with stir-fried slices of chicken breast, sweet corn and mild green chiles.

  1 tablespoon vegetable oil
  1 pound boneless, skinless chicken breast meat, thinly sliced
  1 cup (1 small) quartered, sliced onion
  1 package (1.5 ounces) ORTEGA Burrito Seasoning Mix
  1 cup water
  1 cup whole kernel corn
  ½ cup (4-ounce can) ORTEGA Diced Green Chiles
  8 to 10 (8-inch) soft taco-size flour tortillas, warmed
     Vegetable oil
     ORTEGA Garden Style Salsa, mild (optional)
     ORTEGA Green Chile Guacamole (recipe page 123) (optional)

HEAT oil in large skillet over medium-high heat. Add chicken and onion; cook, stirring constantly, for 3 to 4 minutes or until chicken is no longer pink. Stir in burrito seasoning mix, water, corn and chiles. Bring to a boil. Reduce heat to low; cook, stirring occasionally, for 3 to 4 minutes or until mixture is thickened. Place ⅓ cup chicken mixture on each tortilla; fold into burritos (see tip page 86).

ADD oil to 1-inch depth in medium skillet; heat over high heat for 3 to 4 minutes. Place 1 or 2 burritos in oil; fry, turning frequently with tongs, for 1 to 2 minutes or until golden brown. Place on paper towels to soak. Repeat with remaining burritos.

SERVE warm with salsa or guacamole. Makes 8 to 10 servings.

Quick & E
Mexican

Turkey Tacos (top) (recipe page 83)
Baja Fish Tacos (bottom) (recipe page 81)

asy Cooking

A memorable meal doesn't have to be time-consuming and complicated. Many Mexican favorites, such as tacos, burritos and crisp tostadas, go together in minutes. Instead of laboring over the stove, linger around the table.

When you're in the mood for tacos with a twist, try one of these quick-fix recipes. Choose from fish tacos with a tangy sour cream and cilantro sauce, a turkey and vegetable taco piled high with cheese or tasty soft-shell ground beef tacos.

Taco Dinner

Baja Fish Tacos
~ or ~
Fajita-Style Beef Soft Tacos
~ or ~
Turkey Tacos

Mexicali Corn Salsa

Ortega Refried Beans

Strawberries Topped with Lemon Yogurt

Baja Fish Tacos
TACOS DE PESCADO

Thousands of miles of coastline in Mexico's Baja region mean fresh seafood to prepare in countless ways, such as these fish tacos topped with a sour cream-cilantro sauce.

½ cup sour cream
½ cup mayonnaise
¼ cup chopped fresh cilantro
1 package (12) ORTEGA Taco Dinner Kit (taco shells, taco seasoning mix,
   taco sauce), shells warmed
1 pound (about 4) cod or other whitefish fillets, cut into 1-inch pieces
2 tablespoons vegetable oil
2 tablespoons lemon juice
5 cups shredded cabbage
1½ cups chopped tomato
   Lime wedges (optional)

COMBINE sour cream, mayonnaise, cilantro and *2 tablespoons* seasoning mix in small bowl. Set aside.

COMBINE fish, oil, lemon juice and *remaining* seasoning mix in medium bowl; pour into large skillet. Cook, stirring constantly, over medium-high heat for 4 to 5 minutes or until fish flakes easily when tested with fork.

DIVIDE fish mixture, cabbage and tomato evenly into taco shells. Top with sour cream sauce. Serve with lime wedges and taco sauce. Makes 6 servings.

A Taco Buffet

When you have a taquisa (taco party), you can join in on the festivities because your guests fill their tacos to their own liking.

   Have both crispy corn taco shells and soft flour tortillas warmed and on hand. Then, let your guests choose from a variety of fillings: shredded beef, pork or chicken; different varieties of refried beans; a vegetable filling, such as fried potatoes and zucchini with chiles; crisp, cool garnishes, such as shredded lettuce, diced tomatoes, sliced radishes, sliced green onions, sliced ripe olives and fresh cilantro; an assortment of shredded and crumbled cheeses; sour cream and guacamole; and, of course, a range of salsas to satisfy all tastes, from mild to fiery.

Fajita-Style Beef Soft Tacos

Just as in fajitas, quick-seared onion and green or red bell pepper strips add color and flavor to these flour tortilla soft tacos.

    1 tablespoon vegetable oil
    3 cups (2 medium) green or red bell pepper strips
 1¼ cups (1 medium) quartered, sliced onion
    1 pound ground beef
    1 package (10) ORTEGA Soft Taco Dinner Kit (flour tortillas, taco
        seasoning mix, taco sauce), tortillas warmed
   ¾ cup water

HEAT oil in large skillet over medium-high heat. Add bell peppers and onion; cook, stirring occasionally, for 3 to 5 minutes or until tender. Remove from skillet; set aside. Add meat to skillet; cook, stirring occasionally, for 4 to 5 minutes or until no longer pink. Drain.

STIR in taco seasoning mix, water and bell pepper mixture. Bring to a boil. Reduce heat to low; cook, stirring occasionally, for 5 to 6 minutes or until mixture is thickened.

PLACE ½ cup meat mixture and desired amount of taco sauce on each tortilla; roll up. Makes 10 servings.

Mexicali Corn Salsa

Salsa de Elote

Corn and bell peppers can transform salsa into a distinctive, multi-colored side dish. Make extra and store it in the refrigerator to toss into mixed salad greens.

 1¾ cups (16-ounce jar) ORTEGA Thick & Chunky Salsa, hot, medium or
        mild, or Garden Style Salsa, medium or mild
 1⅓ cups whole kernel corn
   ¼ cup finely chopped green bell pepper
   ¼ cup finely chopped red bell pepper
    2 tablespoons chopped fresh cilantro (optional)

COMBINE salsa, corn, bell peppers and cilantro in medium bowl; cover. Chill for at least 2 hours.

SERVE as a relish with meat or poultry, or as a dip with tortilla chips. Makes 3 cups.

Salsas: Classic to Creative

There is indeed a particular allure to the simple but seemingly magical combination of tomatoes, onions, garlic, chiles, cilantro—and sometimes a little lime juice and olive oil—that make up the classic salsa Mexicana (or pico de gallo, as it is known in the north of Mexico).

This salsa is often served with fresh tortillas or tortilla chips, grilled meats and fish, melted cheese, tacos and tostadas. While the classic salsa remains most prevalent in both Mexico and the United States, there are many other varieties of salsa worth trying.

You can choose from salsas verdes (green sauces) made with green chiles and tomatillos; fiery, smoky salsas made with chipotles (dried, smoked jalapeños); and contemporary interpretations of classic pico de gallo that incorporate additional vegetables or fruits or well-seasoned black beans. The corn salsa opposite is just such a creation.

Turkey Tacos
TACOS DE PAVO

With convenient boneless, skinless turkey breasts, these tacos can be ready in minutes.

     1 tablespoon vegetable oil
     1 cup (1 small) sliced onion
     1 cup (1 small) sliced red or green bell pepper
     1 pound boneless, skinless turkey breast meat, cut into strips
     1 package (1.25 ounces) ORTEGA Taco Seasoning Mix
    ¾ cup water
     2 tablespoons sour cream
     1 package (12) ORTEGA Taco Shells, warmed
     1 cup (1 medium) chopped tomato
  1½ cups (6 ounces) shredded cheddar cheese
       ORTEGA Thick & Smooth Taco Sauce, mild

HEAT oil in large skillet over medium-high heat. Add onion and bell pepper; cook, stirring occasionally, for 3 to 4 minutes or until vegetables are tender. Add turkey; cook, stirring occasionally, for 4 to 5 minutes or until turkey is no longer pink in center.

STIR in seasoning mix and water. Bring to a boil. Reduce heat to low; cook, stirring occasionally, for 5 to 6 minutes or until mixture is thickened. Stir in sour cream.

FILL each taco shell with ⅓ cup turkey mixture; top with tomato, cheese and taco sauce. Makes 6 servings.

Warming Taco Shells

Tacos are made two ways: with corn tortillas and with flour tortillas. Ortega corn tortillas are generally used in crisp tacos; Ortega flour tortillas are generally used in soft tacos. Both kinds of shells taste best when they're warmed before filling.

To warm soft tacos in a microwave oven, wrap a stack of tortillas in waxed paper. To make them even softer, lightly sprinkle each one with water before wrapping. Microwave on HIGH (100%) power for 45 seconds. To heat in a conventional oven, wrap tortillas in aluminum foil. Sprinkle tortillas with water, if desired. Bake in preheated 300°F. oven for 15 minutes.

To warm crisp taco shells, place shells on large microwave-safe plate. Microwave on HIGH (100%) power for 1 minute. For crisper shells, rearrange; heat for additional 30 seconds. Or, place taco shells on baking sheet. Bake in preheated 350°F. oven for 6 to 8 minutes.

Treat your family to an easy Mexican meal with

any of these boldly seasoned burrito recipes.

Bursting with meat, tortillas taste terrific when served with Ortega

Refried Beans and a dessert of sliced tropical fruit.

Family-Pleasing Burritos

Carne Asada Burritos

~ or ~

Burritos Grandes

~ or ~

The Original Burrito

Ortega Salsa

Ortega Refried Beans

Sliced Fresh Mangoes and Bananas

Carne Asada Burritos
(recipe page 86)

Carne Asada Burritos

Carne asada simply means "grilled meat," and it is a favorite in Mexico. In this carne asada recipe, beef skirt or flank steak is rubbed with a spice mixture, quickly cooked, then thinly sliced.

    5 cups Mexican Rice (recipe page 51)
 1¼ to 1½ pounds beef skirt or flank steak
    1 package (1.5 ounces) ORTEGA Burrito Seasoning Mix
 1¾ cups (1-pound can) ORTEGA Refried Beans, warmed (optional)
   10 (10-inch) burrito-size flour tortillas, warmed
       ORTEGA Thick & Chunky Salsa (optional)
       Sour cream (optional)
       Chopped fresh cilantro (optional)

PLACE meat between two pieces of plastic wrap; pound meat with meat mallet or rolling pin to tenderize. Rub burrito seasoning mix on both sides of meat. Broil 5 to 6 inches from heat for 6 to 8 minutes on each side or until desired doneness. Cool for 5 minutes. Cut into thin ½-inch pieces.

SPREAD about 2 tablespoons refried beans on each tortilla. Top each with ½ cup meat and ½ cup rice mixture; fold into burritos (see tip below). Garnish with salsa, sour cream and cilantro. Makes 10 servings.

Folding Burritos

Folding a burrito is like creating an envelope. To fill and fold a burrito, place about ⅓ cup of filling in the center of a flour tortilla. Fold the bottom third of the tortilla up over the filling. Take the left side of the tortilla (that has no filling on it), and fold it over the filling. Repeat with the right side of the tortilla. Then roll up to enclose the filling, forming an easy-to-eat packet.

Burritos Grandes

These super-size burritos are packed with savory ground beef, refried beans, salsa and cheese to satisfy even the heartiest appetite.

> **1 pound ground beef**
> **1 package (1.5 ounces) ORTEGA Burrito Seasoning Mix**
> **1⅓ cups water**
> **1¾ cups (1-pound can) ORTEGA Refried Beans with Green Chiles & Lime, warmed**
> **6 (10-inch) burrito-size flour tortillas, warmed**
> **¾ cup ORTEGA Thick & Chunky Salsa, mild**
> **¾ cup (3 ounces) shredded Monterey Jack or cheddar cheese**

COOK beef in large skillet over medium-high heat, stirring occasionally, for 4 to 5 minutes or until no longer pink; drain. Stir in burrito seasoning mix and water. Bring to a boil. Reduce heat to low; cook, stirring occasionally, for 3 to 4 minutes or until thickened.

SPREAD about ¼ cup beans on each tortilla. Top each with ⅓ cup meat filling, 2 tablespoons salsa and 2 tablespoons cheese; fold into burritos (see tip opposite page). Makes 6 servings.

The Original Burrito

EL BURRITO ORIGINAL

Simple to make, this classic burrito is also delicious made with ground turkey instead of ground beef. Serve with a side of warmed Ortega Refried Beans.

> **1 pound ground beef**
> **1 package (8) ORTEGA Burrito Dinner Kit (tortillas, burrito seasoning mix)**
> **1⅓ cups water**
> **1 cup shredded lettuce**
> **2 cups (8 ounces) shredded cheese**
> **2 cups (2 medium) chopped tomatoes**
> **ORTEGA Thick & Chunky Salsa, medium or mild**

COOK beef in medium skillet over medium-high heat, stirring occasionally, for 4 to 5 minutes or until no longer pink; drain. Stir in burrito seasoning mix and water. Bring to a boil. Reduce heat to low; cook, stirring occasionally, for 5 to 6 minutes or until mixture is thickened.

REMOVE tortillas from outer plastic package. Microwave tortillas on HIGH (100%) power for 10 to 15 seconds or until warm or heat each tortilla in small skillet over medium-high heat, turning frequently, until warm.

SPREAD meat mixture over tortillas. Top with lettuce, cheese, tomatoes and salsa. Fold into burritos (see tip opposite page). Makes 8 servings.

The Cooking of El Norte

The burrito epitomizes the cooking of what Mexicans call El Norte (The North), an 1,800-mile stretch of land that runs from the Pacific coast of Baja California to the lowlands of the Gulf of Mexico. This ranch-style food is hearty and simple and showcases the region's flavorful beef. It is the cooking of El Norte that is most familiar to Americans. Wheat-flour tortillas are a northern twist on the corn tortilla burrito wrapper.

Norteños like to wrap one of their distinctive flour tortillas around their famous beef, spiced with their favorite Ortega chiles.

Invite friends over after a concert or game for sensational tostadas.

Prepare your choice of tostadas topped with either bay shrimp marinated

in a tomato-and-green-chile sauce or refried beans, olives and avocado.

Or, serve both mouthwatering combinations.

Tostada Supper

Ortega Salsa with Tortilla Chips

Shrimp Tostadas
~ *or* ~
Refried Bean Tostadas

White Rice with Green Chiles and Tomatoes

Mixed Greens Salad

Fresh Strawberries and Pineapple Chunks

Shrimp Tostadas
(recipe page 90)

Shrimp Tostadas
TOSTADAS DE CAMARÓN

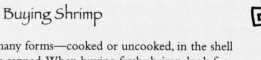

Think of these elegant tostadas as a main-dish salad layered with tomatoes, tiny shrimp and crisp lettuce flavored with green chiles, cilantro and lime juice.

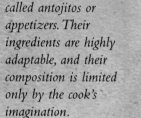

Tostadas

Tostadas fall into a genre of Mexican cuisine called antojitos or appetizers. Their ingredients are highly adaptable, and their composition is limited only by the cook's imagination.

In Mexico, tostadas can be anything from 4-inch miniatures topped with a spicy mixture for an appetizer, to larger tostadas piled higher for a quick, light main meal.

Most Mexicans eat their tostadas outdoors and on the run. Tostadas are among the most popular street foods in Mexico, because of their nearly endless variety. It also helps that the tostada shell serves as an easy-to-hold edible plate.

```
   1  pound cooked bay shrimp
1¾  cups (14.5-ounce can) CONTADINA Dalla Casa Buitoni Recipe Ready
        Diced Tomatoes, drained
   1  cup (1 small) chopped onion
  ½  cup (4-ounce can) ORTEGA Diced Green Chiles
  ¼  cup chopped fresh cilantro
   3  tablespoons vegetable oil
   3  tablespoons lime juice
1¾  cups (1-pound can) ORTEGA Refried Beans with Spicy Jalapeños
   1  package (10) ORTEGA Tostada Shells, warmed
2½  cups shredded romaine lettuce
       Crumbled queso fresco or feta cheese (optional)
       Lime wedges (optional)
```

COMBINE shrimp, tomatoes, onion, chiles, cilantro, oil and lime juice in medium bowl; cover. Chill for 1 to 2 hours or until flavors are blended.

SPREAD about 2 tablespoons beans over each tostada shell. Top each with ¼ cup lettuce and ½ cup shrimp mixture. Serve with cheese and lime wedges. Makes 10 servings.

Buying Shrimp

You can buy shrimp in many forms—cooked or uncooked, in the shell or peeled, fresh, frozen or canned. When buying fresh shrimp, look for those that are moist, firm, fresh-smelling and have translucent flesh. Uncooked and cooked fresh shrimp are both available in the shell, or already peeled and deveined. Frozen shrimp can be raw or cooked, either in the shell or peeled and deveined. Cooked, peeled shrimp also is available canned.

To peel and devein shrimp, open the shell down the underside. Starting at the head, pull back the shell. Gently pull on the tail to remove. Use the tip of a sharp knife to remove the black vein that runs along the center of the back. Rinse the shrimp in cold running water.

To cook 1 pound of shrimp, bring 4 cups water and 1 teaspoon salt to a boil in medium saucepan. Add shrimp. Bring to a boil; reduce heat to low. Cook, uncovered, for 1 to 3 minutes or until shrimp turn pink. Drain. Rinse shrimp under cold water. Serve or chill until ready to use.

Refried Bean Tostadas
TOSTADAS DE FRIJOLES

Making refried beans from scratch would add hours of preparation time to this recipe. Ortega Refried Beans add flavor, without the extra time.

- 1¾ cups (1-pound can) ORTEGA Refried Beans
- ¼ cup chopped onion
- 1 package (1.25 ounces) ORTEGA Taco Seasoning Mix
- 1 package (10) ORTEGA Tostada Shells, warmed
- 2 cups shredded lettuce
- ½ cup (2 ounces) shredded cheddar cheese
- ⅓ cup sliced ripe olives
- 2 medium ripe avocados, cut into 20 slices
- ¾ cup ORTEGA Thick & Smooth Taco Sauce, hot, medium or mild

COMBINE beans, onion and taco seasoning mix in medium saucepan. Cook, stirring frequently, for 4 to 5 minutes or until heated through.

SPREAD ¼ cup bean mixture over each tostada shell. Top with lettuce, cheese, olives, avocado and taco sauce. Makes 10 servings.

White Rice with Green Chiles and Tomatoes
ARROZ BLANCO CON CHILES VERDES Y TOMATES

Although this recipe contains mild green chiles, there are versions of "white rice" recipes infused with fiery serrano or jalapeño peppers that defy their mild appearance.

- 1 tablespoon vegetable oil
- 1 cup long-grain white rice*
- 1 cup (1 small) chopped onion
- 2 cups water
- 1 cup (1 medium) chopped tomato
- ½ cup (4-ounce can) ORTEGA Diced Green Chiles
- 1 teaspoon salt

HEAT oil in medium saucepan over medium-high heat. Add rice and onion; cook, stirring frequently, for 2 to 3 minutes or until onion is tender and rice is slightly golden. Add water; cover. Bring to a boil. Reduce heat to low; cook for 15 to 20 minutes or until most of liquid is absorbed.

STIR in tomato, chiles and salt; heat through. Makes 4 servings.

*NOTE: For quick-cook rice, use 2 cups instant rice instead of 1 cup long-grain white rice. After it comes to a boil, cook for length of time recommended on instant rice package.

Chase away the cold-weather chills with a bowl of one of these tasty soups. Both the full-bodied bean soup and the spicy corn-and-tomato combo are delicious complements to either of these distinctive quesadillas.

Warming Soup Supper

Green Chile Quesadillas
~ *or* ~
Fajita Quesadillas

Creamy Bean Soup
~ *or* ~
Spicy Tomato and Corn Soup

Mixed Greens with Oranges and Jicama

Sugar Cookies

Green Chile Quesadillas
Creamy Bean Soup
(recipes pages 94 and 95)

Green Chile Quesadillas

QUESADILLAS DE CHILES VERDES

Sweet corn and mild green chiles add color and crunch to this cheese-filled snack. For an extra flavorful treat, try using Monterey Jack cheese, cheddar cheese and queso fresco.

   2 cups (8 ounces) shredded cheddar or Monterey Jack cheese or crumbled
    queso fresco
   1 cup (7-ounce can) ORTEGA Diced Green Chiles
   1 cup whole kernel corn
   6 (8-inch) soft taco-size flour tortillas
    ORTEGA Thick & Chunky Salsa, mild (optional)

COMBINE cheese, chiles and corn in medium bowl. Spread 1 cup cheese mixture on one tortilla; place second tortilla evenly over mixture.

PLACE quesadilla in medium skillet well sprayed with nonstick cooking spray. Cook over medium-high heat for 2 to 3 minutes on each side or until golden brown and cheese is melted. Repeat with remaining ingredients. Serve with salsa. Makes 6 servings.

Fajita Quesadillas

Two favorites join forces in this dish—fajita-style chicken and vegetables—to make up this cheesy quesadilla. Top these hot-from-the-griddle quesadillas with cooling Ortega Thick & Chunky Salsa.

   2 tablespoons vegetable oil, *divided*
   1 cup (1 small) quartered, sliced onion
   1 cup (1 small) green or red bell pepper strips
   1 pound boneless, skinless chicken breast meat, cut into strips
   1 package (1.25 ounces) ORTEGA Fajita Seasoning Mix
   ⅓ cup water
   10 (6-inch) fajita-size flour tortillas, *divided*
   2½ cups (10 ounces) shredded cheddar or Monterey Jack cheese, *divided*

HEAT *1 tablespoon* oil in large skillet over medium-high heat. Add onion and bell pepper; cook, stirring occasionally, for 3 to 4 minutes or until vegetables are tender. Add chicken; cook, stirring occasionally, for 4 to 5 minutes or until chicken is no longer pink. Stir in fajita seasoning mix and water; bring to a boil. Reduce heat to low; cook, uncovered, for 3 to 4 minutes or until mixture is thickened.

SPREAD ½ cup chicken fajita mixture on one tortilla; sprinkle with ½ *cup* cheese. Place second tortilla evenly over mixture. Heat *remaining* oil in large skillet over medium-high heat. Place quesadilla in skillet; cook for 2 to 3 minutes on each side or until golden brown and cheese is melted. Repeat with remaining ingredients. Makes 5 servings.

Tortillas: Corn vs. Flour

Fresh tortillas are made and consumed in great quantities every day throughout Mexico. They may be prepared with either masa harina (dried-corn flour) or wheat flour.

What is the main difference between flour and corn tortillas? The ingredients. Corn tortillas may use white, yellow, blue or red corn flour. Flour tortillas contain fat. Traditionally, this has been in the form of lard, but now it's usually vegetable shortening.

The technique for making both types of tortillas is basically the same. The ingredients are mixed into a dough which is pinched into balls, patted or rolled, then cooked on a hot griddle until the tortillas are puffed and golden.

Tortillas can range in size from a mere 2 inches—which are usually fried and topped with beans, meat or cheese as a snack—to 10 inches, which are best stuffed with hearty fillings for a meal.

Creamy Bean Soup
SOPA DE FRIJOLES CON CREMA

This thick and creamy soup is a welcomed sight on a chilly night. Serve it with warmed flour or corn tortillas.

    1 tablespoon vegetable oil
    1 cup (1 small) chopped onion
    4 cloves garlic, finely chopped
 3½ cups (*two* 1-pound cans) ORTEGA Refried Beans
 1¾ cups (16-ounce jar) ORTEGA Thick & Chunky Salsa, mild
 1¾ cups (14½-ounce can) chicken broth
    1 tablespoon lime juice
    2 teaspoons ground cumin
  ½ teaspoon ground red pepper
      Shredded Monterey Jack cheese (optional)
      Chopped fresh cilantro (optional)

HEAT oil in large saucepan over medium-high heat. Add onion and garlic; cook, stirring occasionally, for 2 to 3 minutes or until onion is tender.

STIR in beans, salsa, broth, lime juice, cumin and pepper. Bring to a boil. Reduce heat to low; cook, stirring occasionally, for 10 to 12 minutes. Sprinkle with cheese and cilantro before serving. Makes 6 to 8 servings.

Spicy Tomato and Corn Soup
SOPA PICANTE DE TOMATO Y MAÍZ

The cotija cheese called for in this recipe is just one kind of "queso añejo," or aged cheese, that is perfect for crumbling over a dish. Queso añejo is available at most Mexican markets. If you can't find it, use a dry farmer's cheese or even feta cheese.

 3½ cups (*two* 14½-ounce cans) chicken broth
 2½ cups (about 5 ears) fresh or frozen corn kernels
 2½ cups (24-ounce jar) ORTEGA Thick & Chunky Salsa, medium
  ½ cup (4-ounce can) ORTEGA Diced Green Chiles
  ½ teaspoon salt
    1 cup milk (optional)
  ½ cup (2 ounces) crumbled cotija or feta cheese

COMBINE broth, corn, salsa, chiles and salt in large saucepan. Bring to a boil. Reduce heat to low; cook, stirring occasionally, for 5 to 6 minutes or until corn is crisp-tender. Add milk; cook for 1 to 2 minutes or until heated through. Sprinkle with crumbled cheese before serving. Makes 6 to 8 servings.

For a change of pace, serve your family this creative play on traditional fajitas. The tortillas are filled with an enticing combination of black beans and other vegetables. Pair them with a luscious layered tortilla casserole and you'll satisfy everyone's appetite.

Vegetarian Fajita Dinner

Vegetarian Fajitas

Chilaquiles

Mexican Rice
(recipe page 51)

Lettuce with Avocado and Radish Slices

Fruit Sherbet

*Vegetarian Fajitas
(recipe page 98)*

Vegetarian Fajitas
FAJITAS VEGETARIANAS

Bursting with bright colors, crisp textures and fresh flavors, this meatless version of the favorite sizzling recipe will please everyone from the most health-conscious eater to the most dedicated meat lover.

  1 **tablespoon vegetable oil**
  1 **cup (1 small) quartered, sliced onion**
  1 **cup (1 small) red, green or yellow bell pepper strips**
 1¾ **cups (15-ounce can) black, pinto or kidney beans, rinsed, drained**
  ½ **cup whole kernel corn**
  1 **package (1.25 ounces) ORTEGA Fajita Seasoning Mix**
  ⅓ **cup water**
  ¼ **cup chopped fresh cilantro or parsley**
  6 **(6-inch) fajita-size flour tortillas, warmed**

HEAT oil in large skillet over medium-high heat. Add onion and bell pepper; cook, stirring occasionally, for 3 to 4 minutes or until vegetables are tender.

STIR in beans, corn, fajita seasoning mix and water; bring to a boil. Reduce heat to low; cook, uncovered, for 3 to 4 minutes or until mixture is thickened. Remove from heat; stir in cilantro.

SERVE fajita mixture with tortillas. Makes 6 servings.

Cooking Fresh Corn

Corn in any of its many supermarket forms—fresh, frozen or canned—works in most recipes calling for corn, but there is no doubt that fresh corn from the cob has the truest, sweetest corn flavor.

Look for corn on the cob that still has its husk. A healthy-looking husk tells you the corn is fresh. Store the corn in the husk in the refrigerator for no more than 2 days to retain as much of the sweetness as possible.

To prepare fresh corn, remove the husks from the ears, then scrub with a stiff brush to remove the silks or fibers, then rinse. Cut the kernels from the cob with a sharp knife. Cook, covered, in a small amount of salted boiling water for 4 minutes. Or, steam for 4 to 5 minutes. Drain and serve.

Chilaquiles

This cheesy tortilla casserole can be served for brunch with eggs and refried beans.

    Vegetable oil
12 **(6-inch) corn tortillas, cut into 1-inch strips★**
 1 **cup (1 small) chopped onion**
1¾ **cups (16-ounce jar) ORTEGA Thick & Chunky Salsa, mild**
1¼ **cups (10-ounce can) ORTEGA Enchilada Sauce**
1½ **cups (6 ounces) shredded Monterey Jack or cheddar cheese**
 ¼ **cup ORTEGA Pickled Jalapeño Slices**
    Sour cream (optional)
    Sliced avocado (optional)

ADD oil to 1-inch depth in medium skillet; heat over high heat for 3 to 4 minutes. Place tortilla strips in oil; fry, turning frequently with tongs, until light golden brown. Remove from skillet; place on paper towels to soak.

REMOVE all but 1 tablespoon oil from skillet. Add onion; cook, stirring occasionally, for 1 to 2 minutes or until tender. Stir in salsa and enchilada sauce. Bring to a boil. Reduce heat to low; cook, stirring frequently, for 3 to 4 minutes.

LAYER *half* of tortilla strips in ungreased 13 x 9-inch baking dish. Top with *half* of salsa mixture and *half* of cheese; repeat layers. Bake in preheated 350°F. oven for 10 to 15 minutes or until cheese is melted. Top with jalapeños, sour cream and avocado just before serving. Makes 8 servings.

★NOTE: The frying step may be eliminated by breaking ORTEGA Taco Shells or ORTEGA Tostada shells into small pieces and using them in place of tortilla strips.

Comfort Food

Chilaquiles was created by thrifty cooks looking for a creative way to use leftovers. Its ingredients and method may vary from region to region, as well as from cupboard to cupboard. Although chilaquiles was once referred to as a "poor man's dish," today it is eagerly enjoyed by everyone.

Tempting kids to eat their vegetables is no problem with this meatless menu. Stuffed with cheese and vegetables and served with a robust chile-and-garlic relish, the plump tortilla rolls are sure to become family favorites.

Vegetarian Enchilada Dinner

Ortega Green Chile Guacamole with Tortilla Chips
(recipe page 123)

Spinach and Mushroom Enchiladas

Ortega Green Chiles with Garlic and Oil

Mixed Greens with Dressing

Vanilla Ice Cream with Caramel Sauce

Spinach and Mushroom Enchiladas
Ortega Green Chiles with Garlic and Oil
(recipes pages 102 and 103)

Spinach and Mushroom Enchiladas
ENCHILADAS DE ESPINACA Y HONGO

These fresh-flavored, garden-style enchiladas are perfect as a meatless meal, or whenever you crave something a little out of the ordinary.

1 tablespoon vegetable oil
1 cup (1 large) peeled chopped carrot
½ cup chopped onion
1 clove garlic, finely chopped
3 cups (1 large bunch) chopped fresh spinach or 1 package (10 ounces) frozen chopped spinach, thawed
2 cups (6 ounces) sliced fresh mushrooms
2 cans (10 ounces *each)* ORTEGA Enchilada Sauce, *divided*
¼ to ½ cup vegetable oil
12 (6-inch) corn tortillas
1½ cups (6 ounces) crumbled cotija cheese or shredded Monterey Jack cheese

HEAT 1 tablespoon oil in large skillet over medium-high heat. Add carrot, onion and garlic; cook, stirring frequently, for 3 to 4 minutes or until carrot is crisp-tender. Add spinach and mushrooms; cook for 2 to 3 minutes or until spinach is cooked and mushrooms are soft. Stir in *½ cup* enchilada sauce. Pour *remaining* enchilada sauce into small skillet; heat until warm.

HEAT ¼ cup oil in separate small skillet over medium-high heat for 2 to 3 minutes. Pass tortillas, using tongs, through oil to soften; add more oil as needed. Place on paper towels to soak. Pass tortillas through enchilada sauce in skillet.

PLACE ¼ cup vegetable mixture and about 1 tablespoon cheese down center of each tortilla; roll up. Place seam-side down in 12 x 7-inch baking dish. Top with *remaining* enchilada sauce; sprinkle with *remaining* cheese. Bake in preheated 350°F. oven for 10 to 12 minutes or until heated through and cheese is melted. Makes 6 servings.

Ortega Green Chiles with Garlic and Oil
CHILES VERDE ORTEGA CON AJO Y ACEITE

The Ortega name is synonymous with innovation, as illustrated by the many inventive ways the family served their beloved chiles. Serve this Ortega-family recipe alongside chilled chicken, tossed with greens or tucked into a cold sandwich.

  2 cans (7 ounces *each*) ORTEGA Whole Green Chiles, cut into strips
¼ cup extra virgin olive oil
  2 large cloves garlic, finely chopped
½ teaspoon salt

COMBINE chiles, oil, garlic and salt in medium bowl; cover. Chill for 2 to 4 hours or overnight until flavors are blended. Makes 6 servings.

Quick Ortega Chile Ideas

Keep cans of Ortega Whole Green Chiles and Ortega Diced Green Chiles on hand to dress up your favorite foods. Try some of these ideas:

• Make a warm chile-cheese dip by adding ½ cup (4-ounce can) Ortega Diced Green Chiles to your favorite cheese sauce. For a spicier dip, add 1 teaspoon of Ortega Diced Jalapeños.

• Add ½ cup (4-ounce can) Ortega Diced Green Chiles to mashed potatoes, or spice them up even more with Ortega Diced Jalapeños.

• For an easy omelet filling, use Ortega Whole Green Chiles and Monterey Jack cheese as the filling.

• Add Ortega Diced Green Chiles or Diced Jalapeños to mayonnaise and use as a sandwich spread.

• For a quick and easy dip for vegetables, add ½ cup (4-ounce can) Ortega Diced Green Chiles to an 8-ounce container of sour cream. Add garlic salt to taste.

• To prepare an "Ortega burger," top a grilled burger with Ortega Whole Green Chiles and a slice of Monterey Jack or cheddar cheese.

• Slice Ortega Whole Green Chiles and add to salads, soups or casseroles.

• Use Ortega Whole Green Chiles inside quesadillas, grilled cheese sandwiches, meat sandwiches or enchiladas.

• For a simple but elegant meal, top a grilled chicken breast with Ortega Whole Green Chiles and Monterey Jack cheese, then heat briefly to melt the cheese.

Chiles

The cultivation and consumption of chiles in Mexico go back to the ancient Aztecs and Mayans, who not only appreciated chiles for their unique flavor, but also because they thought chiles had nutritive and medicinal value.

The sharp flavor of chiles is captured by their original Indian name, "tzir"—which means "to pierce."

Accent on the Ho

Tamales (recipe page 108)
Zucchini with Green Chiles (recipe page 110)